THE PROPHETS SPEAK OF HIM

THE PROPHETS SPEAK
OF HIM

Encountering Jesus in the Minor Prophets

ANTHONY T. SELVAGGIO

SERIES EDITORS
DR JOHN D. CURRID AND ROBERT STRIVENS

EVANGELICAL PRESS

 EVANGELICAL PRESS

Evangelical Press
Faverdale North Industrial Estate, Darlington, DL3 0PH England
email: sales@evangelicalpress.org

Evangelical Press USA
PO Box 825, Webster, NY 14580 USA
email: usa.sales@evangelicalpress.org

www.evangelicalpress.org

First published 2006

 The EMMAUS series has been created to speak directly to pastors, teachers and students of the Word of God on those issues that impact on their everyday ministry and life

British Library Cataloguing in Publication Data available

ISBN-13 978 0 85234 612 9   ISBN 0 85234 612 3

Contents

INTRODUCTION

THE MINOR PROPHETS ARE AN IMPORTANT but often neglected part of the Bible. The corpus which constitutes the Minor Prophets includes twelve books written by twelve different prophets. Due to the number of books, they were historically referred to as 'The Book of the Twelve' or simply 'The Twelve'. Today, they are most commonly referred to as the 'Minor Prophets'. It is important to note, however, that they are not referred to as 'minor' because they lack theological significance, but this title rather reflects the relatively short length of their individual prophecies. In fact, these twelve books are anything but minor. They are filled with tremendously deep and rich theological material. The Minor Prophets will certainly not prove minor to any reader who will invest the time to explore them.

The Minor Prophets cover a period of about 300 years. Hosea, the first of the twelve, began his prophetic ministry around 750 B.C. and Malachi, the last of the twelve, delivered his message around 460 B.C. This 300-year period included numerous significant events in the history of Israel and Judah.[1] During this period great empires arose and met their demise, including Assyria and Babylon. The people of God experienced major invasions and deportations. They endured the pain of exile and experienced the joy of restoration. The Minor Prophets also deal with very significant biblical themes such as God's love, the work of the Spirit of God, the Day of the Lord and the kingdom of God. Finally, the Minor Prophets speak to a variety of other issues including politics, social justice and business ethics.

While the Minor Prophets speak to a vast array of issues, this book is particularly focused on what they have to say about Jesus Christ. This book is not a verse-by-verse commentary on the Minor Prophets, nor is it an effort to deal with all of the implications of their prophecies. Rather, this book is about how the Minor Prophets speak about Jesus Christ. Why is the focus on Jesus Christ? It is because Jesus is the central figure of the entire Bible. The entire Bible speaks of him, including the Minor Prophets. Simply stated, the Bible is ultimately about Jesus Christ and his redemptive work. Jesus made this very claim to his followers.

Jesus had several interesting encounters with his disciples after the resurrection. Two of these are described at the end of Luke's Gospel. Luke informs us that Jesus first met two disciples on the road to Emmaus (Luke 24:13-32) and then later encountered the eleven apostles (Luke 24:32-53). In both cases, Jesus found his followers discouraged and confused about his crucifixion. He patiently explained to them that his death and resurrection were taught in the Old Testament. At one point, he told the apostles: 'This is what I told you while I was still with you: Everything must be fulfilled that is written about me in the Law of Moses, the Prophets and the Psalms' (Luke 24:44). Jesus was saying that the Old Testament speaks about him. The purpose of this book is to see how one segment of the Old Testament, the Minor Prophets, speaks of Jesus Christ and his redemptive work.

While seeing Jesus in the Old Testament is a laudable goal, it is not without its pitfalls. Often the attempt to see Jesus in the Old Testament has resulted in a practice known as 'allegorizing'. Allegorizing is a method of interpretation which views biblical persons, places, events or things without regard to their literal, historical and contextual meanings. The allegorical method is more interested in finding hidden spiritual meanings in these things. Often these meanings are found by making fanciful comparisons (or allegories) between an Old Testament person, place, event or thing and Jesus Christ. This type of interpretation dominated the church from the third to the sixteenth century.[2] The Reformation led the move away from the allegorical method; however, the allegorical method is not ancient history. It continues to be employed in pulpits today. Perhaps you have heard a sermon employing this method.

The problem with the allegorical method is that it often results in unwarranted and outlandish interpretations of the Old Testament. Take for instance the following text from Exodus: 'Then Moses cried out to the LORD, and the LORD showed him a piece of wood. He threw it into the water, and the water became sweet. There the LORD made a decree and a law for them, and there he tested them' (Exod. 15:25). One famous nineteenth-century preacher contended that the piece of wood in this text represented the cross of Christ and that the river represented the human soul. His sermon emphasized the fact that just as the piece of wood rendered the bitter water sweet, so too the cross of Christ sweetens the human soul.[3] While it is true that Christ sweetens the human soul, this truth is not taught by Exodus 15:25. In the end, the allegorical method undermines the Bible by allowing the expositor to make connections which, however interesting, are not supported by the text. It is my goal to avoid the error of the allegorical method in this book.

The best way to avoid this error, and other errors of biblical interpretation, is to adhere to sound principles of interpretation. What follows is a brief description of three principles which will guide our study of the Minor Prophets.[4] Think of them as navigational devices which will help us to remain on course as we endeavour to see Jesus in the Minor Prophets.

First, the safest and most reliable way to see Jesus in the Minor Prophets is through explicit New Testament references which directly link the words of the Minor Prophets to his person and work. For example, in Matthew 2:15 the gospel writer states that Hosea 11:1, 'When Israel was a child, I loved him, and out of Egypt I called my son', is a reference to Jesus Christ. As you will recall, Joseph and Mary had to flee to Egypt when Jesus was an infant in order to avoid the persecution of King Herod. Matthew, under the inspiration of the Holy Spirit, informs us that this event occurred in order to fulfil this prophecy of Hosea. In other words, Matthew tells us that Jesus is the Son who comes out of Egypt; he informs us that Hosea was ultimately speaking about Jesus. This principle, because of its inspired nature, will serve as the main guiding principle of this book. Therefore, as we examine each minor prophet, I will note significant citations of the prophet's message in the New Testament.

A second way to see Jesus in the Minor Prophets is through an interpretative tool known as 'typology'. Typology is a way to draw connections between the Old Testament and the New Testament by recognizing legitimate analogies and parallels. Like the first principle, this principle is also found in the Bible itself. Many of the New Testament writers employ this very method of interpretation. For example, Paul understood Adam as a type of Christ noting that Adam 'was a pattern of the one to come' (Rom. 5:14).[5] The writer to the Hebrews describes the Old Testament tabernacle as a type of the heavenly tabernacle: 'For Christ did not enter a man-made sanctuary that was only a copy of the true one; he entered heaven itself, now to appear for us in God's presence' (Heb. 9:24). Jesus notes that the brazen serpent which Moses lifted up in the desert was a type of his own crucifixion (John 3:14). As you can see from these examples, a type may involve a person (Adam), place (tabernacle), thing (brazen serpent) or event (the lifting up of the serpent and subsequent healing of the people in Numbers 21).

In addition, the examples cited above reveal another aspect of typology. In typology, the 'antitype' (the New Testament fulfilment of the type) far exceeds the glory and import of the original type in the Old Testament. This principle is known as 'escalation' and it reminds us that the New Testament realities far outshine their Old Testament shadows. Clearly, the heavenly tabernacle is superior to the earthly tabernacle and Christ is superior to both Adam and the brazen serpent.

Before we leave this topic, let me make one final point regarding typology. The examples of typology cited above all involve a direct and explicit typological connection made by the Bible itself. Sometimes, however, there are typological connections which are not as biblically explicit as these examples, but which are still genuine types worthy of our attention. It is often the case, particularly in prophetic literature, that a legitimate type may be inferred from the totality of revelation even though no explicit connection is made by the Bible. For example, I will argue that the prophet Hosea's relationship to his unfaithful wife Gomer serves as a type of Christ's relationship to his bride, the church.[6]

To summarize this second principle, let me give you the following helpful and concise definition of typology from I. Howard Marshall: 'Typology may be defined as the study which traces parallels or correspondences between incidents recorded in the OT and their counterparts in the NT such that the latter can be seen to resemble the former in notable respects and yet to go beyond them.'[7] As we journey through the Minor Prophets, I will attempt to point out significant typological connections between their messages and Jesus Christ.

A third way to see Christ in the Minor Prophets is by recognizing the biblical themes which appear both in the writings of the prophets and in the work of Christ. Sidney Greidanus illustrates this method by using the example of the biblical theme of ransom.[8] In the Old Testament a ransom had to be paid to deliver Israel from Egypt (Exod. 12:13) and to free slaves (Lev. 25:47-49). In the New Testament, Jesus describes his ministry in terms of a ransom: 'For even the Son of Man did not come to be served, but to serve, and to give his life as a ransom for many' (Mark 10:45).

Another example is the theme of repentance. The prophet Joel, like many of the minor prophets, called on the people of God to repent of their sins. In the New Testament, repentance becomes one of the central themes of Jesus' preaching ministry. In fact, as we will see when we study Joel's prophecy, the New Testament reveals that Jesus grants the repentance called for by Joel (Acts 5:31). As we survey the Minor Prophets, I will draw your attention to major biblical themes which connect the Minor Prophets to Jesus Christ.

These are the three principles which will guide our study of the Minor Prophets. It is important to point out that these three principles are united by one common presupposition, namely that the Bible is a progressively unfolding book which comes to its crescendo and fulfilment in the New Testament with the person and work of Jesus Christ. That is the ultimate purpose of this book, to see how the messages of the Minor Prophets speak of Jesus Christ and his redemptive work.

In conclusion, I want to make two other points about this book. First, this book is intended to provide you with an *introduction* to the ways in which Christ is seen in the Minor Prophets. This book is not an exhaustive treatment of the Minor Prophets, but rather it is a selective work which is intended to acquaint the reader with some ways in which these powerful books point to the Messiah. In other words, this book will not deal with every aspect of Christ in the Minor Prophets. Second, and most importantly, I want to emphasize that this book is not merely a clever attempt to connect the dots from the Minor Prophets to Jesus Christ. Rather, the goal of this book is to exalt the Lord Jesus Christ and to call the reader to serve him. The following comment from John Stott on the topic of preaching aptly captures this ultimate goal: 'The main objective of preaching is to expound Scripture so faithfully and relevantly that Jesus Christ is perceived in all his adequacy to meet human need ... The preacher's purpose is more than to unveil Christ; it is to unveil him so that people are drawn to come to him and receive him.'[9] This book is an effort to 'unveil Christ' from the words of the Minor Prophets so that you will be 'drawn to come to him and receive him'.

Chapter 1

INCOMPARABLE LOVE: HOSEA

CERVANTES' NOVEL, *Don Quixote*, is a humorous and satirical story about the adventures of an eccentric Spanish knight. Don Quixote travels around Spain wearing rusty armour and riding an old broken-down horse. During his quest to express his knightly chivalry he encounters a variety of imagined enemies. Don Quixote is one of the most memorable and beloved characters in Western literature, but while I find Don Quixote intriguing, my favourite character in Cervantes' novel is Don Quixote's loyal companion, Sancho Panza. Sancho, who is aware of his master's eccentricities, nevertheless remains loyal to him throughout his ridiculous journey. I suppose I greatly admire the qualities Sancho exemplifies, namely loyalty and commitment.

Western culture is currently facing a crisis of commitment. We see it in our divorce rates, we see it in our churches and we see it in the business world. We are in a here today, gone tomorrow culture. When the going gets tough, we just get going. Thankfully, God is not like that. God does not break his promises. He keeps his commitments, even at tremendous cost. The book of Hosea reminds us of God's commitment to his people. Hosea teaches us that despite our infidelity God continues to love us with an incomparable love because of Jesus Christ.

ENTERING INTO HOSEA'S WORLD

Hosea began his ministry in the early part of the eighth century B.C. His ministry extended over a long period of time. The very first verse of the book informs us that he prophesied during the reigns of four kings of Judah: Uzziah, Jotham, Ahaz and Hezekiah. It is likely that he ministered for fifty or sixty years. His influence was widespread, impacting both parts of the divided kingdom – Israel and Judah. When he began his ministry Israel and Judah were peaceful and prosperous, but there were problems looming.

Socially, there was a growing gap between rich and poor, a breakdown in public morality and a corrupt legal system. God described the state of the culture as follows: 'There is only cursing, lying and murder, stealing and adultery; they break all bounds, and bloodshed follows bloodshed' (Hosea 4:2).

Politically, turmoil arose when King Jeroboam's son, Zechariah, was assassinated in 745 B.C. after sitting on the throne for only six months. In the following twelve years, five different kings would come to rule Israel and four of them would be assassinated. In addition to the internal social and political turmoil, Israel was under constant fear of invasion from what was then the world's greatest empire – Assyria. In 722 B.C., after Hosea's prophetic ministry had ended, Israel was, in fact, conquered by the Assyrians and the people of Israel were deported.

To make matters worse, the religious condition of the people of Israel was even more dire than their social and political situations. God had entered into a covenant with Israel, but they were violating the sacredness of this covenant relationship in every way. The people were idolatrous: 'Though Ephraim built many altars for sin offerings, these have become altars for sinning' (Hosea 8:11). They also ignored God's law: 'I wrote for them the many things of my law, but they regarded them as something alien' (Hosea 8:12). The people were living in utter unfaithfulness: 'Hear the word of the LORD, you Israelites, because the LORD has a charge to bring against you who live in the land: "There is no faithfulness, no love, no acknowledgment of God in the land"' (Hosea 4:1). Hosea describes the nation as having '…A spirit of prostitution … [I]n their heart; they do not acknowledge the LORD' (Hosea 5:4). This was the context in which Hosea was called to minister. He was called to serve a corrupt society and an unfaithful church. For nearly sixty years he was called to be God's mouthpiece, to confront a nation spiralling into decay.

AN INDECENT PROPOSAL?

As if that wasn't a difficult enough task, God asked Hosea to do something even more extraordinary. 'When the LORD began to speak through Hosea, the LORD said to him, "Go, take to yourself an adulterous wife and children of unfaithfulness, because the land is guilty of the vilest adultery in departing from the LORD"' (Hosea 1:2). God asked Hosea to marry an adulterous woman! Although there are some differences of opinion among biblical scholars, I believe that Hosea was called to marry a woman who was already an adulterer, not one who would later become an adulterer. This woman is referred to as an adulteress not because she had one lapse into sexual indiscretion, but rather because her whole life was marked by adultery. John Calvin described Hosea's wife as follows: '…for he speaks not here of an unchaste woman only, but of a woman of wantonness, which means a common harlot … who has long habituated herself to wantonness, who has exposed herself to all, to gratify the wish of all, who has prostituted herself, not once, nor twice, nor to few men, but to all.'[1] You get the picture; Hosea's wife is the epitome of sexual infidelity.

And it gets even worse for Hosea. For God not only required Hosea to marry an adulterous woman, but when she proves her unfaithfulness after they are married, he is required to go after her:

> The LORD said to me, 'Go, show your love to your wife again, though she is loved by another and is an adulteress. Love her as the LORD loves the Israelites, though they turn to other gods and love the sacred raisin cakes.' So I bought her for fifteen shekels of silver and about a homer and a lethek of barley. Then I told her, 'You are to live with me many days; you must not be a prostitute or be intimate with any man, and I will live with you' (Hosea 3:1-3).

Do you see what's going on here? Hosea marries Gomer and she eventually leaves him to continue practicing her adultery. She ends up being sold as a slave. So does God say to Hosea, 'Let her go, she's getting what she deserves'? No, to the contrary, God commands Hosea to go and buy her back!

Now just pause and think about this for a moment. Hosea is being asked to walk into the town square and buy his wife back at an auction. Do you know how a woman slave was sold at an auction? All of her clothes were removed so that the buyers could see the merchandise. Hosea had to bear the indignity of entering into a crowd of men gazing at his undressed wife. If that was not enough, he also had to bid for her! He had to bid for his own wife! Imagine that scene for a moment, Hosea offering competing bids against other men until he finally wins the auction by bidding fifteen shekels and ten bushels of barley. Hosea now owns his wife. He has bought her back with a price. Imagine the shame of that day as he took his wife off the auction block and through the crowd of knowing onlookers.

Why did God make Hosea endure such personal hardship? It is because God transmitted his message not only through Hosea's words, but through his life as well. He used the life of Hosea to get the attention of the people. Just imagine the news of Hosea's marriage travelling through Israel. Everyone would have heard of this scandal – a prophet marrying a harlot! This is great fodder for the tabloids of the time. Can you imagine the shame that Hosea experienced? Remember, many of the men would have known Gomer intimately. Can you imagine what it was like for Hosea to walk in the streets – the glaring looks he would receive, the knowing smiles from unrighteous men, and the scorn-filled gazes of the self-righteous? Hosea's marriage was certainly an attention-grabber!

Hosea was not only asked to preach a message, but he was also asked to bear that message in his very flesh in order to wake up the world around him. He was commanded and sent by God to be a living spectacle. God used Hosea as an object lesson. He was trying to teach Israel that *they* were Gomer, the unfaithful and adulterous wife.

Now we understand what Hosea's message meant in his time, but that does not answer the broader question. How does Hosea fit into redemptive history? In other words, what does Hosea say to us? What does it mean to us? Is it a manual for maintaining a good marriage?

Is it an admonition to keep your commitments in life? Is it a moral lesson against prostitution and sexual infidelity? No, it was primarily given to show us Jesus Christ, to speak of him! But how does Hosea speak of Jesus? The prophecy of Hosea speaks of Jesus in two ways. First, it reveals to us that Jesus is the faithful husband and, second, that he is the faithful son.

JESUS IS THE FAITHFUL HUSBAND

As we have seen, Hosea's prophecy is rife with condemnations of Israel's adultery. Just as Hosea's wife Gomer continually prostitutes herself, so too does Israel. But in the midst of these condemnations of Israel is the promise that God, as marriage-Lord of Israel, as Israel's husband, will one day pursue and beautify his bride: 'Therefore I am now going to allure her; I will lead her into the desert and speak tenderly to her. There I will give her back her vineyards, and will make the Valley of Achor a door of hope. There she will sing as in the days of her youth, as in the day she came up out of Egypt' (Hosea 2:14-15). Furthermore, God promised not only to pursue his bride, but to betroth her forever and give her gifts like righteousness and faithfulness: 'I will betroth you to me forever; I will betroth you in righteousness and justice, in love and compassion. I will betroth you in faithfulness, and you will acknowledge the LORD' (Hosea 2:19-20). Hosea contains a promise of a restored marriage wherein the adulterous bride is rendered holy, righteous and faithful.

However, as I mentioned in the beginning of this chapter, Israel falls to the Assyrians in 722 B.C. This promised transformation does not take place during Hosea's lifetime. In fact, it does not occur during the remaining history of the Old Testament. Israel continues to be an unfaithful bride. So the question must be asked: was Hosea's prophecy ever fulfilled? Did God ever pursue his bride? Did he ever bestow on her righteousness and holiness? The answer is *yes*! He did it through the faithful husband Jesus Christ.

The New Testament tells us that the church is betrothed to Christ. Jesus spoke of his ministry as that of a bridegroom coming for his bride (Matt. 25:1-13, Mark 2:19-20). The apostle Paul also connects Christ's relationship to the church with the marital relationship (Eph. 5:25). However, the New Testament speaks of a two-stage process in the church's marriage to Christ. In this present age, the church is betrothed to Christ (2 Cor. 11:2) and it is only after the return of Christ that our marriage will be fully consummated (Rev. 19:7-9). However, it is important to keep in mind that the concept of betrothal in the first century is very different from the modern concept of marital engagement. In first century Jewish culture, to be betrothed to another was a more serious commitment than it is today. Biblical commentator William Hendriksen describes the seriousness of first century betrothal: 'Betrothal among the Jews must not be confused with present-day engagement. It was far more serious and binding. The bridegroom and bride pledged their troth to each other in the presence of witnesses. In a *restricted sense* this was essentially the marriage.'[2] Mary and Joseph provide us with a powerful biblical example of the seriousness of betrothal. Mary was betrothed to Joseph and during this period of betrothal she became pregnant by the power of the Holy Spirit. When Joseph first learned of Mary's pregnancy he assumed that she had been unfaithful and Matthew records his thoughts: 'Because Joseph *her husband* was a righteous man and did not want to expose her to public disgrace, he had in mind to *divorce her* quietly' (Matt. 1:19, emphasis mine). Although Mary and Joseph were not yet married, Matthew speaks of Joseph as Mary's 'husband' and Joseph contemplates 'divorce' to deal with what he thinks is infidelity on Mary's part. As you can see, in the first century a betrothed couple was essentially a married couple. All that remained future for a betrothed couple was the wedding feast, the physical consummation of their marriage and dwelling together permanently. Therefore, although the marital relationship between Christ and the church is not fully consummated until Christ's return, it is proper to consider the church the bride of Christ in this present age, for we are betrothed to him. Christ is truly our husband. Having laid that foundation, let's see how the relationship between Hosea and Gomer functions as a type of Christ's relationship to the church.

As previously noted, Hosea's relationship to his unfaithful bride Gomer analogically expressed God's relationship with his unfaithful bride Israel. When we read Hosea we learn of a husband who had to bear the reproach of his wife's unfaithfulness. Hosea reveals to us that God's incomparable love for his wayward bride includes bearing her reproach. Like Hosea, Jesus endured humiliation to buy his wife back. He bore the reproach and shame of our sinfulness (Isa. 53:4-5). He bore the shame of the cross on our behalf: 'Let us fix our eyes on Jesus, the author and perfecter of our faith, who for the joy set before him endured the cross, scorning its shame, and sat down at the right hand of the throne of God' (Heb. 12:2). Like Hosea, Jesus bore the reproach of his wayward bride.

However, if you think about it, Jesus went even further than Hosea. Hosea was required to go into the marketplace and pay for Gomer, but Jesus, when he came for us, paid a much higher price, at a much greater personal cost. He gave *himself* as the price! 'For there is one God and one mediator between God and men, the man Christ Jesus, who gave himself as a ransom for all men – the testimony given in its proper time' (1 Tim. 2:5-6). Hosea paid fifteen shekels and ten bushels of barley, but the cost to Jesus was his very life!

In addition, while Hosea bore the shame of having an un-righteous bride, Jesus, in essence, became the unfaithful bride for us. You could say he became Gomer for us. He was stripped and made a public spectacle for us. He was paraded through the streets of Jerusalem for us. Greater yet, Jesus did something that Hosea could never do for his bride; Jesus bore the sins of his bride and gave her his righteousness: 'God made him who had no sin to be sin for us, so that in him we might become the righteousness of God' (2 Cor. 5:21). Jesus is the faithful husband who transforms the harlot – *you* – into a wife who is holy and blameless.

Do you see the practical joys of having Jesus as your husband? In a culture in which fidelity is so hard to find, where spouses so often abandon one another, Jesus is forever faithful. He promises never to leave or forsake his beloved bride (Heb. 13:5). He not only remains faithful to his bride, but he also adorns her with his holiness. One of my great joys as a husband is to purchase my wife a gift which enhances her beauty. For example, it brings me great pleasure to see her radiantly adorned with a new dress. This small earthly gesture, however, pales in comparison to the work of our heavenly husband, for the new dress with which Jesus adorns his bride is nothing other than his own resplendent holiness! Paul makes this very connection in his epistle to the Ephesians:

> Husbands, love your wives, just as Christ loved the church and gave himself up for her to make her holy, cleansing her by the washing with water through the word, and to present her to himself as a radiant church, without stain or wrinkle or any other blemish, but holy and blameless (Eph. 5:25-27).

The apostle John tells us that on the Last Great Day we will indeed be a suitable and holy bride: 'I saw the Holy City, the new Jerusalem, coming down out of heaven from God, prepared as a bride beautifully dressed for her husband' (Rev. 21:2).

In Jesus, the prophecy of Hosea 2:19-20 is fulfilled, for Jesus betroths us forever in righteousness, justice, love, compassion and faithfulness. He is our faithful husband and we can look forward to the day when our marriage to him will be fully consummated. We can look ahead with great anticipation to the wedding supper of the Lamb and the joy of living with him for ever!

JESUS IS THE FAITHFUL SON

The prophecy of Hosea speaks of Jesus in a second way. There are two family relationships explored in the book of Hosea: the husband-wife relationship and the father-son relationship. When people think of Hosea, they often forget the latter.

Hosea speaks about the nation of Israel not only as God's bride, but also as his son. When God called Israel to be a nation, he referred to the nation as his 'son'. This can be seen in God's instructions to Moses: 'Then say to Pharaoh, "This is what the LORD says: Israel is my firstborn son, and I told you, 'Let my son go, so he may worship me.' But you refused to let him go; so I will kill your firstborn son,"' (Exod. 4:22). God refers to this father-son relationship in the prophecy of Hosea: 'When Israel was a child, I loved him, and out of Egypt I called my son' (Hosea 11:1). However, during the time of Hosea's prophecy, Israel had become an unfaithful son, a son who disappointed the Father and a son who rejected the Father's commandments. Hosea describes this in chapter eleven of his prophecy:

> But the more I called Israel, the further they went from me. They sacrificed to the Baals and they burned incense to images. It was I who taught Ephraim to walk, taking them by the arms; but they did not realize it was I who healed them. I led them with cords of human kindness, with ties of love; I lifted the yoke from their neck and

bent down to feed them. Will they not return to Egypt and will not Assyria rule over them because they refuse to repent? (Hosea 11:2-5).

Israel had become an unfaithful son. The more God called to them the further they went away from him. In essence, they had become the prodigal son.

Just as Hosea had to endure an unfaithful wife to teach Israel about its national infidelity, he also had to endure unfaithful children to teach Israel about its prodigal behaviour. At the very beginning of his prophecy, God informed Hosea that he will have 'children of unfaithfulness' (Hosea 1:2). One of these unfaithful children was a son named Lo-Ammi, which means 'not my people'. The name of this son reveals just how far Israel had failed in their calling to be God's son. If you recall, the heart of God's covenant promise to Israel was, 'I will walk among you and be your God, and you will be my people' (Lev. 26:12). Through Hosea's son, Lo-Ammi, God was saying, 'You will not be my people, because you are an unfaithful and disobedient son.'

Here arises the plot tension in the drama of redemption. How is God going to resolve this? He has bound himself through covenant to deliver this nation, this son he called out of Egypt. Remember what he said to them in the Ten Commandments: 'I am the LORD your God, who brought you out of Egypt, out of the land of slavery' (Exod. 20:2). But now his son has gone astray. How can he keep his promise, while simultaneously maintaining his holiness and justice? Will Israel ever receive a new beginning? Will they ever be a faithful son?

The Gospel of Matthew informs us that God kept his promise. Matthew tells us of a new beginning for the people of God. For the angel came to Mary and told her, 'You will be with child and give birth to a son, and you are to give him the name Jesus' (Luke 1:31). And when Herod threatened to kill this son, Mary and Joseph took him to Egypt: 'So he got up, took the child and his mother during the night and left for Egypt, where he stayed until the death of Herod. And so was fulfilled what the Lord had said through the prophet: "Out of Egypt I called my son"' (Matt.

2:14-15, see Hosea 11:1). Israel once again returns to Egypt, but this time Israel is embodied in one representative figure, the Son of God, Jesus Christ – out of Egypt God called his Son!

This is the second way Hosea speaks of Jesus. Jesus is the true Israelite. He is the true Son of God. He is the faithful Son who, unlike disobedient Israel, comes out of Egypt and keeps all of God's commandments and pleases him in every way: 'This is my Son, whom I love; with him I am well pleased. Listen to him!' (Matt. 17:5). Jesus, unlike Israel, faithfully completes the whole course of his calling, so that in his high priestly prayer the Son can proclaim to the Father, 'I have brought you glory on earth by completing the work you gave me to do' (John 17:4). Jesus is the faithful Son of God.

The fact that Jesus is the faithful Son of God has profound implications for those who trust in him, for Jesus, the faithful Son, is able to make *you* a faithful son of God. The apostle Paul, drawing from Hosea, explains how God's father-son relationship with Israel is now broadened to include all those who believe in Jesus Christ:

> As he says in Hosea: 'I will call them "my people" who are not my people; and I will call her "my loved one" who is not my loved one,' and, 'It will happen that in the very place where it was said to them, "You are not my people," they will be called "sons of the living God"' (Rom. 9:25-26).

In Jesus, we who were once not a people, we who were the Lo-Ammi, now become a people: 'Once you were not a people, but now you are the people of God; once you had not received mercy, but now you have received mercy' (1 Peter 2:10). What incomparable love! The apostle John expresses the incomparable nature of the Father's love when he proclaims: 'How great is the love the Father has lavished on us, that we should be called children of God! And that is what we are!' (1 John 3:1). Jesus is the faithful Son who makes *you* a faithful son and fulfils the promise that God will be our God and we will be his people.

INCOMPARABLE LOVE

In the last chapter of the prophecy of Hosea God says of his people: 'I will heal their waywardness and love them freely, for my anger has turned away from them' (Hosea 14:4). This prophecy of Hosea was fulfilled in Jesus Christ. In Jesus our waywardness is healed. In Jesus we freely receive the love of God. In Jesus God's anger is turned away from us. In Jesus we receive incomparable love! That is how Hosea speaks of Jesus.

QUESTIONS FOR DISCUSSION

1. Read Ephesians 5:22-32 and list all of the things that Christ does for his bride, the church.

2. What are some of the broken promises that people experience in this world? Discuss how God's faithfulness to his promises can be used to minister to people who have experienced the pain of broken promises.

3. This chapter emphasizes what Christ has done for us in making us a beautiful bride and a faithful son. However, there are also imperatives (commands) for us that flow from this glorious work of Christ on our behalf. Discuss the nature of these imperatives as revealed in the following texts: 2 Corinthians 6:18 – 7:1, Ephesians 5:1-16 and 1 John 3:1-3. Can you think of other passages which teach similarly?

4. In this chapter we have seen that Jesus makes us sons in God's family. This doctrine is referred to as the doctrine of adoption. Read the following verses and list all the benefits which result from our adoption by God: Psalm 103:13, Proverbs 14:26, Matthew 6:30-32, Romans 8:15, Galatians 4:6, Hebrews 12:5-6 and 1 Peter 5:7.

Chapter 2

A CALL FOR RADICAL REPENTANCE: JOEL

THE PROLIFIC ENGLISH WRITER CHARLES DICKENS created many memorable characters including Oliver Twist and David Copperfield, but perhaps his most famous character is Ebenezer Scrooge. Scrooge, of course, is that miserly fellow in Dickens' *A Christmas Carol*. In that story, Dickens describes Scrooge as:

> a squeezing, wrenching, grasping, scraping, clutching, covetous old sinner! Hard and sharp as flint, from which no steel had ever struck out generous fire, secret, and self-contained, and solitary as an oyster ... He carried his own low temperature always about with him; he iced his office in the dog days, and didn't thaw it one degree at Christmas.[1]

A Christmas Carol is a story about Scrooge's transformation from a greedy, selfish and cold-hearted man to a man of generosity, joy and warmth. It is a story of repentance – radical repentance. However, Scrooge's repentance did not occur spontaneously or without an intervening force. His repentance required a wake up call in the form of three ghosts. Scrooge required a shocking experience to awaken his cold heart from its slumber.

The book of Joel tells a similar story of repentance. The prophet Joel was sent to wake up a nation of Scrooges, to make them recognize that they required radical repentance. It is this call for repentance which continues to make Joel's message relevant today, for we too need radical repentance.

ENTERING INTO JOEL'S WORLD

Little is known about Joel's historical setting. It is even difficult to pinpoint the general time period of his prophecy. Fortunately, knowledge of the exact historical setting is not a prerequisite for understanding Joel. The themes he deals with are transcendent and timeless. There is, however, one historical fact that we do know from Joel, a fact which is essential for comprehending the prophet's mission and message. Joel informs us that during his ministry Judah experienced two agricultural disasters.

First, their crops were ravaged by swarms of locusts which came in successive waves: 'What the locust swarm has left the great locusts have eaten; what the great locusts have left the young locusts have eaten; what the young locusts have left other locusts have eaten' (Joel 1:4). Second, they were hit with a crippling drought:

The seeds are shriveled beneath the clods. The storehouses are in ruins, the granaries have been broken down, for the grain has dried up. How the cattle moan! The herds mill about because they have no pasture; even the flocks of sheep are suffering. To you, O LORD, I call, for fire has devoured the open pastures and flames have burned up all the trees of the field. Even the wild animals pant for you; the streams of water have dried up and fire has devoured the open pastures (Joel 1:17-20).

Judah had been hit with two crushing blows in the form of locusts and drought. These disasters were unlike anything Judah had experienced before: 'Hear this, you elders; listen, all who live in the land. Has anything like this ever happened in your days or in the days of your forefathers?' (Joel 1:2). Judah was driven to its knees and Joel used these disasters as metaphors in his prophetic message. Joel told the people that God was using locusts and drought to get their attention. Much like the ghosts who visited Scrooge, these disasters were sent to awaken the people of Judah to their need for repentance.

THE HEART OF THE PROBLEM

When Judah experienced these two devastating disasters they likely thought that these were their biggest problem. However, Joel tells them that the locusts and drought were only signs pointing to a larger, more significant problem. They had a religious problem, a problem of the heart. Their hearts were far from the Lord. They had fallen into apostasy and idolatry. They had forgotten that Jehovah was their God. They had given their hearts to other gods.

Although the book of Joel does not contain a direct charge of idolatry, we can deduce that this was at the core of the problem through two pieces of evidence. First, we have God's description of how Judah will behave after they repent: 'Then you will know that I am in Israel, that I am the LORD your God, and that there is no other' (Joel 2:27). Based on this statement, it seems clear that their problem was following other gods. The second piece of evidence is the meaning of the name of the prophet himself. The name 'Joel' means 'Jehovah is God'. The people needed to be reminded that Jehovah was their God and there was no other. Judah's problem was that the hearts of the people were far from the Lord. Their behaviour was a violation of God's covenant and there are always consequences for such a violation.

Deuteronomy 28 clearly outlines a pattern of blessings and cursings. The first fourteen verses express how God will reward Israel for their obedience. The remaining verses in this chapter delineate the curses for disobedience. Included among the acts of disobedience which will trigger the curses is the act of 'following other gods' (v. 14). Interestingly, both locusts (28:38-42) and drought (28:23-24) are listed among the curses for disobeying God. Judah was experiencing the consequences of their covenant disobedience.

However, Joel informs the people of Judah that the locusts and drought are nothing in comparison to the judgement that God will send if they refuse to repent. Joel tells them that the locusts and drought are harbingers of a greater judgement to come, a judgement which Joel calls 'the day of the Lord': 'Alas for that day! For the day of the LORD is near; it will come like destruction from the Almighty' (Joel 1:15). In effect, Joel was saying to them, 'You think locusts are bad? You think a drought is rough? Well, you ain't seen nothing yet!' Listen to how Joel describes this day:

> Blow the trumpet in Zion; sound the alarm on my holy hill. Let all who live in the land tremble, for the day of the LORD is coming. It is close at hand – a day of darkness and gloom, a day of clouds and blackness. Like dawn spreading across the mountains a large and mighty army comes, such as never was of old nor ever will be in ages to come. Before them fire devours, behind them a flame blazes. Before them the land is like the garden of Eden, behind them, a desert waste – nothing escapes them (Joel 2:1-3).

Joel describes the day of the Lord in terms of a military invasion and what makes the description of this invasion even more horrific for the people of Judah is the fact that God is the general of the invading army: 'The LORD thunders at the head of his army; his forces are beyond number, and mighty are those who obey his command. The day of the LORD is great; it is dreadful. Who can endure it?' (Joel 2:11).

Do you see what is going on? Judah is depicted as being ravaged on the day of the Lord. That's a big plot twist for Judah. In their minds, that's not how things are supposed to play out. One can imagine a citizen of Judah saying, 'Uh, wait a minute here God. This day of the Lord thing is for those other people. We are Judah. We are your chosen people. That fire and brimstone stuff is for your enemies.' It is true that the day of the Lord is for God's enemies, but the bad news for Judah was – they had become God's enemy.

God sent locusts, a drought and the prophet Joel to Judah in order to wake them up to the impending judgement. The good news for Judah was that there was a way to avoid the devastation of the day of the Lord – radical repentance:

> 'Even now,' declares the LORD, 'return to me with all your heart, with fasting and weeping and mourning.' Rend your heart and not your garments. Return to the LORD your God, for he is gracious and compassionate, slow to anger and abounding in love, and he relents from sending calamity (Joel 2:12-13).

The only way that the people of Judah could avoid the destruction of the day of the Lord was to repent. However, the question that arises is: How can fallen men and women ever provide the type of radical repentance called for by the prophet Joel? It is with this question that Joel turns our eyes to Jesus.

JESUS MAKES REPENTANCE POSSIBLE

The call to radical repentance is not just a central theme in the prophecy of Joel. It is also a central part of the ministry of Jesus. At the beginning of his earthly ministry, Jesus declared that calling sinners to repentance was at the core of his work: 'I have not come to call the righteous, but sinners to repentance' (Luke 5:32). At the end of his earthly ministry, on the road to Emmaus, Jesus declared that calling sinners to repentance would be a continuing mark of his church: 'This is what is written: The Christ will suffer and rise from the dead on the third day, and repentance and forgiveness of sins will be preached in his name to all nations, beginning at

Jerusalem' (Luke 24:46-47). Jesus, like Joel, calls all people to radical repentance. He calls you to radical repentance! However, this drives us back to the question: How can we provide the type of repentance called for by Joel and Jesus?

To discover the answer to this question, we must first come to terms with what we mean by repentance. John Murray (1898-1975) described repentance as follows:

> Repentance consists essentially in change of heart and mind and will. The change of heart and mind and will principally respects four things: it is a change of mind respecting God, respecting ourselves, respecting sin, and respecting righteousness. Apart from regeneration our thought of God, of ourselves, of sin, and of righteousness is radically perverted. Regeneration changes our hearts and minds; it radically renews them. Hence there is a radical change in our thinking and feeling. Old things have passed away and all things have become new.[2]

It is clear from Murray's definition that true repentance is only possible after we are radically changed by the work of regeneration. Repentance requires that we first be regenerated by the Spirit of God. We see this lesson taught in the Scriptures in the encounter between Jesus and Nicodemus recorded in John 3.

Early in his earthly ministry Jesus had an encounter with a Pharisee named Nicodemus. Nicodemus was no average Pharisee. Rather, he was a member of the Jewish ruling council, and therefore, he was well schooled in the Scriptures. One night Nicodemus sought out Jesus and said to him, 'Rabbi, we know you are a teacher who has come from God. For no one could perform the miraculous signs you are doing if God were not with him' (John 3:2). Here Nicodemus seems to offer a partial confession of the Lordship of Christ, but his confession seems to suggest that believing in Jesus is not a radical step, that it requires no real change in him. In his reply, Jesus drives right to the heart of the matter: 'I tell you the truth, no one can see the kingdom of God unless he is born again' (John 3:3). Nicodemus then asks Jesus how it is that a man can be born again. Jesus answers that this new birth is by the power of the Spirit: 'I tell you the truth, no one can enter the kingdom of God unless he is born of water and the Spirit' (John 3:5). The first act of repentance, the act of turning from sin to God, requires a radical change wrought by the Spirit of God.

This connection between the act of repentance and the work of the Spirit is evident in the prophecy of Joel. In the very same chapter in which Joel calls for repentance, he also speaks of the promise of the coming of the Holy Spirit in a new and mighty way:

> And afterward, I will pour out my Spirit on all people. Your sons and daughters will prophesy, your old men will dream dreams, your young men will see visions. Even on my servants, both men and women, I will pour out my Spirit in those days (Joel 2:28-30).

This prophecy was fulfilled in the New Testament on the day of Pentecost (Acts 2:16-18). On that day Peter explained the extraordinary events by stating, 'This is what was spoken by the prophet Joel' (Acts 2:16). The Holy Spirit, who was intimately involved in the original creation (Gen. 1:2), came on the day of Pentecost to begin the work of the new creation.[3] And what did the Spirit produce when he came on the day of Pentecost? Three thousand people repented and were baptized (Acts 2:41).

Perhaps you are wondering: What does the work of the Spirit have to do with Jesus? It is important to realize that the Spirit's coming was conditioned upon the completion of Christ's work. Jesus makes this very point in the Gospel of John: 'Up to that time the Spirit had not been given, since Jesus had not yet been glorified' (John 7:39). The day of Pentecost, the new work of the Spirit, was made possible by the death, resurrection and ascension of Jesus Christ. Note how Peter connects the new birth with the resurrection of Christ: 'Praise be to the God and Father of our Lord Jesus Christ! In his great mercy he has given us new birth into a living hope *through the resurrection of Jesus Christ from the dead*' (1 Peter 1:3, emphasis mine). Redemption had to be accomplished

breast and said, "God, have mercy on me, a sinner'" (Luke 18:13).
Here we see an example of what Joel called for in his prophecy.
Remember, the prophet Joel called on the people to rend their
hearts and not their garments (Joel 2:13). When a Hebrew was in
mourning, he would tear his garments to display his internal feel-
ing of sorrow (see Job 1:20), but God is telling us that he doesn't
want just the externals. He desires more than our mere garments.
He desires our hearts! He desires godly sorrow. The tax collector
expresses this by beating his breast and praying for mercy. The Bible teaches us that some people will express real repentance (godly
sorrow) and others will simply express worldly sorrow.

The second element in real repentance is a true change of direction in our lives. The most common Greek word for repentance
in the New Testament is the word metanoia. Metanoia is perhaps
best translated as 'to change one's mind'. Real repentance not only
requires genuine sorrow for our sins, but it also requires us to truly
change our behaviour. Remember, Joel called the people to rend
their hearts and to return to God (Joel 2:13). Real repentance involves a turning away from our sins. It involves a drastic change in
direction. It involves a change in our minds. Isaiah makes this very
point in his prophecy: 'Let the wicked forsake his way and the evil
man his thoughts. *Let him turn to the LORD*, and he will have mercy
on him, and to our God, for he will freely pardon' (Isa. 55:7, emphasis mine). Here Isaiah tells us that the granting of God's pardon
is dependent on forsaking wicked ways and thoughts. Isaiah calls
on the sinner to 'turn to the Lord'. Genuine sorrow is not enough.
Real repentance requires us to turn from our sins; it requires us to
change our minds and our behaviour.

We can see that repentance requires a change in our behaviour
by looking at a couple of examples from the gospels. First, take the
case of Zacchaeus in Luke 19. Zacchaeus was a wealthy tax collector and he became wealthy by overcharging the people. Zacchaeus
desperately wanted to see Jesus so he climbed a tree. Jesus called
to him and then told him that he needed to stay at his house. The
people were bewildered that Jesus would be a guest of a sinner
(Luke 19:7). However, something glorious happened in the life

of Zacchaeus. He was reborn and he immediately repented of his sin: 'But Zacchaeus stood up and said to the Lord, "Look, Lord! Here and now I give half of my possessions to the poor, and if I have cheated anybody out of anything, I will pay back four times the amount"' (Luke 19:8). It was not enough for Zacchaeus to recognize that he was a sinner. It was not enough for Zacchaeus to feel sorrowful about his sin. Real repentance requires a change in behaviour and Zacchaeus displayed this change by returning the money he gained through unjust means.

A second example is that of the rich young ruler who came to Jesus and asked the question, 'What must I do to inherit eternal life?' (Mark 10:17). Jesus confronted him with the law of God in order to work repentance in his heart. However, the rich young ruler clung to his self-righteousness and stated that he had kept all the commandments from his youth (Mark 10:20). Then Jesus confronted the man regarding his unrepentant sin of trusting in his riches: '"One thing you lack," he said. "Go, sell everything you have and give to the poor, and you will have treasure in heaven. Then come, follow me"' (Mark 10:21). Jesus demanded real repentance. He demanded that the rich young ruler demonstrate a change in his behaviour by selling the things he was coveting. Unlike Zacchaeus, however, this man did not express real repentance and left only expressing the worldly sorrow we discussed above: 'He went away sad, because he had great wealth' (Mark 10:22). There was no change in behaviour. There was no real repentance.

As we have seen from these two examples, the Bible teaches us that some people will express real repentance and others will not. Why is this the case? Why can't all people express real repentance? The Bible tells us that real repentance can only come as a gift of God. Paul makes this very point to Timothy when he instructs him about dealing with those who oppose him. Paul admonishes Timothy to gently instruct his opposition, 'in the hope that *God will grant them repentance* leading them to a knowledge of the truth' (2 Tim. 2:25, emphasis mine). Real repentance is a gift of God. In fact, the Bible not only states that real repentance is a gift of God, but it also connects the bestowal of this gift directly to the redemp-

last time you repented – really repented? Is your repentance demonstrative of worldly sorrow or godly sorrow? Does your repentance involve a real change in direction? Are you like Zacchaeus or the rich young ruler? Are you satisfied with a general repentance or do you repent of your sins particularly? Have you heeded the call of Joel to rend your hearts and return to the Lord? Have you heeded the call of Jesus to the woman caught in adultery: 'Go now and leave your life of sin' (John 8:11)? Have you apprehended the inexhaustible riches of mercy that are available to you in Christ? Repentance is a vital part of the Christian life and heaven rejoices when radical repentance is expressed: 'In the same way, I tell you, there is rejoicing in the presence of the angels of God over one sinner who repents' (Luke 15:10). Repentance is an imperative of the Christian life.

The Promise of a Pardon

The book of Joel ends with a hopeful promise that the people of God will be pardoned: 'Their bloodguilt, which I have not pardoned, I will pardon' (Joel 3:21). The pathway to this pardon includes our expression of radical repentance. This radical repentance is made possible, and made real, by the work of Jesus Christ. It is only through Jesus that we can express the radical repentance called for by Joel and it is only through Jesus that we can be pardoned. That is how Joel speaks of Jesus!

Questions for Discussion

1. In the prophecy of Joel, God sent disasters (locusts and drought) to the people to alert them to a coming judgement. Discuss whether you think God still does this in our own time.

2. One of the main sins of the people during Joel's time was idolatry. This idolatry manifested itself through the people's allegiance to false gods. How does idolatry manifest itself in our culture, our churches and your own heart? Identify the false gods of the modern age.

3. The Westminster Confession of Faith calls on believers not to be satisfied with a general repentance of their sins, but instead it

calls them to repent of their 'particular sins, particularly' (chapter 15, section 5). Why is this important?

4. As discussed in this chapter, real repentance includes both genuine sorrow and a change in behaviour. Read the following passages and identify which aspect of real repentance is identified in each:

    a. Psalm 51:13
    b. Psalm 51:4
    c. Luke 15:21-24
    d. Matthew 3:8-10

5. Repentance is not an abstract doctrine which has no bearing on the believer's life. Read Psalm 32 and discuss the ramifications of failing to confess and repent of our sins (see particularly vv. 3-4). Also, note how David describes the status of a believer who has truly repented and experienced forgiveness (vv. 1-2).

said. 'One day you'll see him and another you won't. He doesn't like being tied down – and of course he has other countries to attend to. It's quite all right. He'll often drop in. Only you mustn't press him. He's wild, you know. Not like a tame lion.'[1]

Lewis reminds us that God is no tame lion.

Our popular culture tries to convince us otherwise. Think of how God is portrayed in popular film. Hollywood tells us that God is affable, amicable and even comedic – in other words, a tame lion.

However, it's not just our popular culture that's off the mark. We Christians also so often attempt to domesticate God, treating him like a toothless lion in the idol factories of our hearts. The prophet Amos was called to confront an entire nation which was treating God as a toothless lion. Amos was sent to remind them of his roar. 'The lion has roared – who will not fear? The Sovereign LORD has spoken – who can but prophesy?' (Amos 3:8). Amos reminds us that God is not to be trifled with; he is no tame lion!

ENTERING THE WORLD OF AMOS

The prophetic ministry of Amos took place around the year 760 B.C. Jeroboam II was on the throne of Israel and Assyria was the dominant power of the world. Fortunately for Israel, the Assyrians were occupied with other threats, and therefore, Israel was allowed to expand its territory and wealth. Amos preached to a nation which was experiencing a time of peace and prosperity. An extremely wealthy class had developed and they were enjoying their wealth: 'You lie on beds inlaid with ivory and lounge on your couches. You dine on choice lambs and fattened calves. You strum away on your harps like David and improvise on musical instruments. You drink wine by the bowlful and use the finest lotions...' (Amos 6:4-6). Things were good in Israel, at least for some.

Others did not have it so good. The poor were being abused. They were sold into slavery. Amos accuses the wealthy of 'buying the poor with silver and the needy for a pair of sandals' (Amos 8:6). The poor were being denied justice. Amos states that the wealthy

'…trample on the heads of the poor as upon the dust of the ground and deny justice to the oppressed' (Amos 2:7).

In addition to oppressing the poor, the entire culture was caught up with greed and consumption. They were addicted to the world of commerce; they couldn't wait for the markets to open. The people were saying, 'When will the New Moon be over that we may sell grain, and the Sabbath be ended that we may market wheat?' (Amos 8:5). This intoxication with riches led them to cheat in the marketplace. They were '…skimping the measure, boosting the price and cheating with dishonest scales' (Amos 8:5). Israel was enchanted by luxury and opulence. Commerce and wealth had become their gods.

Of course these social issues impacted the spiritual state of the people. They transformed significant historical sites, such as Bethel and Gilgal, into centres of false worship (Amos 4:4) and when they came to the true house of God their worship was so superficial and perfunctory that God utterly rejected them:

> I hate, I despise your religious feasts; I cannot stand your assemblies. Even though you bring me burnt offerings and grain offerings, I will not accept them. Though you bring choice fellowship offerings, I will have no regard for them. Away with the noise of your songs! I will not listen to the music of your harps (Amos 5:21-23).

The people were disregarding God; they were treating him as a toothless lion.

So this was the state of Israel at the time of Amos – materially well-off, socially unjust and theologically vacuous.

THE PROPHET'S MESSAGE

Now let's shift our setting for a moment. Let's move about ten miles south of Jerusalem to the land of Tekoa. In that region lived

– who will not fear? The Sovereign LORD has spoken – who can but prophesy?'

Amos had a bleak message. Israel would be torn to shreds and face famine and meaninglessness. The end was coming for Israel and the question that arises, the plot tension in the drama of redemption, is: 'Is there any hope?' With this question Amos turns our eyes to Jesus.

JESUS ENDS THE FAMINE

As we have seen, Amos predicted that Israel would experience a time of spiritual famine (Amos 8:11-12). He described a time when men would search for the word of the Lord, but not find it. One of the blessings of the Israelites was that, of all nations, God spoke his special revelation to them. As Paul puts it in Romans, the Israelites were 'entrusted with the very words of God' (Rom. 3:2). However, as Amos prophesied, Israel experienced a time when God's word was difficult to find. For a period of 400 years, God ceased sharing his written word with Israel. From the closing of the book of Malachi to the opening of the book of Matthew there was a great gap of revelatory silence. There was a famine in the land, a famine of the Word of God.

With the birth of Jesus, this famine came to an end. First, there was the revelation to Zechariah and Elizabeth regarding the birth of John the Baptist, the forerunner of the Messiah (Luke 1:5-25). This was followed by the revelation to Mary that she would bear a son named Jesus (Luke 1:26-38). Following this was the revelation to Simeon who held the infant Jesus in the temple and proclaimed, 'Sovereign Lord, as you have promised, you now dismiss your servant in peace. For my eyes have seen your salvation' (Luke 2:29-30). This flurry of revelation continued through the prophetess Anna, a woman who was at the temple day and night praying for the Messiah to come. When she saw Jesus in the temple, she 'gave thanks to God and spoke about the child to all who were looking forward to the redemption of Jerusalem' (Luke 2:38). Next we hear the voice of John the Baptist, the greatest of all the Old Testament prophets: 'Prepare the way for the Lord, make straight paths for him.' God was speaking again! The famine had come to an end, but this was only a foretaste of what was to come.

God ultimately ended the famine of the Word by sending his only begotten Son to us. The Gospel of John reminds us that Jesus is the 'Word' (John 1:1) and that the 'Word became flesh and made his dwelling among us' (John 1:14). Jesus is the Word incarnate. His earthly ministry included the tasks of preaching and teaching the Word of God (Matt. 4:23). He came to proclaim the good news. After hundreds of years of silence, God now speaks voluminously through his Son: 'In the past God spoke to our forefathers through the prophets at many times and in various ways, but in these last days he has spoken to us by his Son' (Heb. 1:1-2).

The coming of Jesus not only ended the famine of the word, but it also ended the famine of meaninglessness. Just as God provided manna for his famished Israelites as they were on their pilgrimage to the Promised Land, so also God sent Jesus as the true manna from heaven to end the famine of his Word and nourish his New Covenant people during their pilgrimage. As Jesus proclaimed in John's Gospel, 'I am the bread of life. He who comes to me will never go hungry, and he who believes in me will never be thirsty' (John 6:35). Jesus satisfies our hunger for meaning.

This famine-ending work of Christ is so vital for our world today. Many of us, particularly in the West, live in proud nations, nations of opulence and luxury, nations of greed and consumption. Israel at least waited until after the Sabbath to resume their consumption and commerce; we do it twenty-four hours a day, seven days a week. In our prosperity, we too have forgotten God. Just like Israel, we too are suffering from meaninglessness. Isn't this the plague of the modern world? A world which did not want God is now struggling to live without him, struggling with questions of being and meaning.

We live among people who are famished for significance. Our response to such a desperate world must be to bring them the true manna from heaven. We are not to hoard this true manna within the walls of our churches, but rather to share it with the world around us. The Great Commission is a call to end the famine by

hands' (Rev. 7:9). Through Jesus, the son of David, people from every nation are blessed.

In Jesus the promises to Abraham and David coalesce in the unfolding of redemptive history. It is no wonder that Matthew commences his Gospel by associating Jesus with these two great covenant figures: 'A record of the genealogy of Jesus Christ the son of David, the son of Abraham' (Matt. 1:1). Jesus builds a new nation in fulfilment of Amos 9:11-12. In fact, the New Testament reveals that the early church understood the nation-building work of Jesus as a fulfilment of this very prophecy from Amos.

One of the major differences between this new nation and Old Testament Israel is that the former includes Gentiles on a broad scale. Certainly, old Israel occasionally brought in Gentile believers, but with this new nation the door to the Gentiles is opened wide. As Paul states in the second chapter of Ephesians, the dividing wall between Jew and Gentile has been removed by the work of Christ and he has made the two into one new man. However, the merging of Jews and Gentiles was no easy task and as this new nation was being built the Bible records the tensions which arose. The friction over the issue of Gentile inclusion came to a head in the fifteenth chapter of the book of Acts. That chapter records that the church leaders met together in a council at Jerusalem to debate this very issue. In the midst of their deliberations, James stood up and stated the following:

> Simon has described to us how God at first showed his concern by taking from the Gentiles a people for himself. The words of the prophets are in agreement with this, as it is written, 'After this I will return and rebuild David's fallen tent. Its ruins I will rebuild, and I will restore it, that the remnant of men may seek the Lord, and all the Gentiles who bear my name, says the Lord, who does these things that have been known for ages.' It is my judgment, therefore, that we should not make it difficult for the Gentiles who are turning to God (Acts 15:14-19).

James ends the debate by quoting from Amos 9:11-12. The church understood that Jesus, in fulfilment of the prophecy of Amos and of the promises to Abraham and David, was building a new nation! Jesus is the shepherd who pulls the nation of Israel from the lion's mouth and out of the torn and tiny remains of that nation he builds a glorious kingdom (Amos 3:12), a kingdom that includes all nations which bear his name: 'And they sang a new song: "You are worthy to take the scroll and to open its seals, because you were slain, and with your blood you purchased men for God from every tribe and language and people and nation. You have made them to be a kingdom and priests to serve our God, and they will reign on the earth"' (Rev. 5:9-10). Jesus restored the fallen tent of David!

The nation-building work of Christ has profound implications for believers. First, Jesus calls you to be a citizen of his kingdom and to place your allegiance to his kingdom above all else. In the Gospel of Matthew, Christ commands us to seek first his kingdom (Matt. 6:33). In Paul's letter to the Philippians, he reminds us that our citizenship is a heavenly citizenship (Phil. 3:20). To be a citizen of this kingdom means ordering your life according to the laws of the King. Second, being a citizen in this new nation brings tremendous benefits and privileges. In the second chapter of Ephesians, Paul informs us that while we were once excluded from citizenship, we are now, through the work of Christ, 'fellow citizens with God's people and members of God's household' (Eph. 2:19). As a citizen of this new nation, you enjoy all the benefits of being a member in Christ's body. You hear the Word of God preached. You receive the sacraments. You enjoy the fellowship and encouragement of other believers. Most of all you enjoy union with Christ. Finally, it is part of your calling to continue the nation-building work of Christ. This work is not over. Christ continues to build this nation by adding new members. You are called to participate in this work by sharing the good news of this kingdom with those who are foreigners and aliens to its promises. Christ has called you to be an agent of his redemptive work of nation-building.

Chapter 4

THE KINGDOM IS THE LORD'S: OBADIAH

HAVE YOU EVER EXPERIENCED THE PAIN OF DEFEAT? Perhaps you were part of a sports team which lost to an underdog in the last minutes of the game. Perhaps you were part of a competitive event in which you finished second. Perhaps you lost your job or failed a class in school. Most of us have experienced some form of personal defeat in our lives. However, defeat can also be experienced on a national level. Imagine what it must have been like to be a French citizen watching the Nazis march through the Arc de Triumph in Paris in World War II. National defeat is a bitter pill to swallow.

Defeat in any form is difficult enough in itself to endure, but the sting of defeat is exacerbated when someone else rejoices over your defeat. In the days of Obadiah, Judah experienced a national defeat at the hands of the Babylonians, and what made this defeat

were in conflict from the moment of conception. Even their parents were in conflict; Isaac preferred Esau and Rebekah preferred Jacob.

This age-old conflict continued to emerge at various times in Israel's history. For example, during Israel's voyage to the Promised Land, the King of Edom denied Israel permission to travel through the country of Edom, thus making their trip more arduous (Num. 20:14-21). The conflict continued to rage after Israel's conquest of Canaan. David conquered Edom for a time (2 Sam. 8:13-14), but the Edomites struck back during the reigns of Jehosophat (2 Chr. 20:1-2) and Jehoram (2 Kings 8:20-22). Later, under King Amaziah, Judah regained the upper hand and severely punished the Edomites, casting many of them off the top of a cliff (2 Chr. 25: 11-12). I hope by now you get the picture. There was a long history of hate between these two nations.

Now let's return to the time of Obadiah. Think about it for a moment. Israel has lost everything. And what do they see? They see the Edomites, their ancient rivals, dancing in the streets! As Psalm 137 records, 'Remember, O LORD, what the Edomites did on the day Jerusalem fell. "Tear it down", they cried, "tear it down to its foundations!"' (Ps. 137:7) This is why God sent Obadiah to declare such harsh judgement against Edom: 'The house of Jacob will be a fire and the house of Joseph a flame; the house of Esau will be stubble, and they will set it on fire and consume it. There will be no survivors from the house of Esau. The LORD has spoken' (Obad. 1:18). However, the prophecy of Obadiah is not entirely about the coming judgement upon Edom; it also contains a promise of future deliverance for Judah.

GOD'S PROMISE TO JUDAH

Following God's complaint against Edom, he speaks words of comfort to his people Judah. In verse 17 he tells them that on 'Mount Zion there will be deliverance' and that 'the house of Jacob [not Esau] will possess its inheritance'. In verse 18 he tells them that 'the house of Jacob will be a fire' and 'the house of Esau will be stubble'. And in verse 21 he comforts his people by telling them that Mount Zion will rule over the mountains of Edom.

Clearly, Obadiah makes a contrast between Mount Zion and Mount Edom. It's important to know a bit of topography to fully understand the import of this contrast. The cliffs of Edom were as high as 5,000 feet 1,524 metres and their rocky cliffs kept them safe from invaders. Therefore, Edom took great pride in their mountains. Obadiah describes this pride in his prophecy: 'The pride of your heart has deceived you, you who live in the clefts of the rocks and make your home on the heights, you who say to yourself, "Who can bring me down to the ground?"' (Obad. 1:3). God promised through Obadiah that Mount Zion would triumph over the mountains of Edom, that the current situation would not stand, and that in the future the kingdom would be the Lord's (Obad. 1:21).

These are great promises of comfort to Judah, but don't forget that when they were spoken Judah was in exile in Babylon. The house of Jacob was desolate – no king, no priests, no temple, no land! From their vantage point, it sure did not look like the kingdom would be the Lord's. In fact, it looked more like Esau had finally triumphed over Jacob. How would the house of Jacob prevail over Edom? How would the kingdom be the Lord's? To answer these questions we must turn our eyes to Jesus.

JESUS IS THE VICTORIOUS SEED

As you recall, God promised a day when the Edomites would become as 'stubble' (Obad. 1:18). He promised that a day would come when there would be 'no survivors from the house of Esau' (Obad. 1:18). This prophecy was fulfilled by the person and work of Jesus Christ. In order to fully comprehend how Christ fulfilled this prophecy we must understand that the conflict between Jacob and Esau, between Edom and Israel, is not ultimately a sibling conflict or a national conflict, but rather it is a spiritual conflict.

Early in this chapter, I mentioned that the rivalry between Israel and Edom goes all the way back to the time of Rebekah. Al-

ment it was born. She gave birth to a son, a male child, who will rule all the nations with an iron scepter. And her child was snatched up to God and to his throne (Revelation 12:4-5).

Vern S. Poythress, in his commentary on Revelation, connects Revelation 12 to the actions of Herod and to the great cosmic battle between Christ and Satan:

> Satan attempts to destroy the child as soon as he is born, as Herod did in Matthew 2:1-18. Herod's action was the first in a series of satanically engineered attempts to prevent the accomplishment of God's salvation. Satan tempted Christ in the wilderness (Matt. 4:1-11; Luke 4:1-14) and was active in the background when Christ cast out demons and confronted opposition from Jewish leaders. Revelation encapsulates all this opposition in the single picture of Satan seeking to devour the child. Passing over Jesus' earthly life, it arrives immediately at the ascension and enthronement of the Messiah: her child was snatched up to God and to his throne.[2]

Jesus not only defeated the Edomite Herod, he not only defeated the earthly seed of the serpent, but he also defeated the serpent himself. Jesus defeated Satan. Jesus is the victorious Seed!

While we can take tremendous comfort and joy in the fulfilment of the prophecy of Obadiah and the victory of Jesus over the seed of the serpent, there remain two warnings for us from this prophecy. The first warning comes from Esau himself. As John Owen pointed out, Esau had all the external privileges of the covenant of grace, yet he was reprobate. To put this in modern parlance, Esau was born into a Christian family, catechized, sent to a Christian school, attended a Christian college and went to church each week. Esau was reared in a Christian home and had all the benefits of living in the covenant community and yet he was an outcast from the covenant of grace! This should be a warning to both children and parents. We cannot rely solely on the outward privileges of the church for salvation.

The second warning comes from the book of Revelation. We know that Jesus has won the victory over Satan. Revelation 12:5 tells us that Jesus ascended into heaven and reigns there: 'And her child was snatched up to God and to his throne.' However, Revelation also tells us that Satan has another target: 'Then the dragon was enraged at the woman and went off to make war against the rest of her offspring – those who obey God's commandments and hold to the testimony of Jesus' (Rev. 12:17). As Poythress notes, 'The Messiah himself is beyond reach of satanic attack. So, subsequent to the ascension, Satan turns his attention to the woman, the followers of the Messiah.'[3] The conflict between the seeds continues to rage in this present age. Our comfort is that the decisive blow has already been rendered by Jesus, but we must continue to keep alert and put on the armour of God (Eph. 6:11-18).

IN JESUS THE KINGDOM IS THE LORD'S

The second major promise given by Obadiah is that 'Deliverers will go up on Mount Zion to govern the mountains of Esau. And the kingdom will be the LORD's' (Obad. 1:21). Most commentators agree that what is envisioned here is much broader than merely having the people of God restored to the land of Judah. In this last verse, Obadiah is speaking about a universal kingdom that will include the whole world. This universal scope of Obadiah's prophecy is hinted at in verse 15: 'The day of the LORD is near for *all nations*' (Obad. 1:15, emphasis mine).

The conclusion of the prophecy of Obadiah can only be fully understood through the kingdom of Jesus Christ. As John Calvin noted, 'It does unquestionably appear that the prophet speaks here of the kingdom of Christ…'[4] The prophetic promise of Obadiah that the 'kingdom will be the Lord's' is fulfilled in the church of Jesus Christ, the primary manifestation of the kingdom of God. Verse 17 of Obadiah's prophecy serves to reinforce this conclusion: 'But on Mount Zion will be deliverance; it will be holy.' The last part of this verse may also be translated, 'there shall be holiness'. Matthew Henry comments on this verse as follows:

> There, upon Mount Zion, in the gospel-church, shall be holiness; for that is it which becomes God's house for-ever, and the great design of the gospel and its grace is to plant and promote holiness. There shall be the Holy Spirit, the holy ordinances, the holy Jesus, and a select remnant of holy souls, in whom, and among whom, the holy God will delight to dwell … Where there is holiness there shall be deliverance.[5]

The church of Jesus Christ is the kingdom of holiness of which Obadiah spoke and Jesus reigns as this kingdom's only King and Head (Eph. 5:23, Col. 1:18). Through the work of Jesus Christ the kingdom is the Lord's!

Choose This Day

The prophecy of Obadiah ultimately tells us about two kingdoms: the kingdom of Christ and the kingdom of Satan. There is no third alternative. There is no neutral ground. You must serve one or the other. Obadiah tells us that Satan's time is short. He tells us that the kingdom will be the Lord's. Revelation 11:15 confirms the fulfilment of the prophecy of Obadiah by stating, 'The king-dom of the world has become the kingdom of our Lord and of his Christ, and he will reign for ever and ever.' The New Testament tells us that when Jesus returns the time for deciding will be over. The time to decide is now. As one commentator put it:

> The dominion long usurped by the prince of this world, and judicially permitted for a time, because of man's sin, shall then cease; 'and the kingdom shall be the Lord's.' What wise man then can hesitate whether to take his por-tion with the world and Satan, or with the Church and Christ?[6]

Which kingdom are you serving? Obadiah calls you to serve the victorious Seed of the woman. He calls you to serve the King of Kings. That's how Obadiah speaks of Jesus.

QUESTIONS FOR DISCUSSION

1. In this chapter we examined the conflict which exists between the Seed of the woman and the seed of the serpent. While Jesus is the conquering Seed, the conflict is not yet over. Discuss some ways in which this conflict is revealed in our society and culture today.

2. Discuss how the following texts relate to the continuing conflict between the Seed of the woman and the seed of the serpent (Acts 9:4; Romans 16:20; Ephesians 6:11-18 and Revelation 12).

3. The Edomites found their confidence in the high cliffs which kept them safe from invaders. This led them to have pride and confidence in themselves rather than God (Obad. 1:3). The seed of the serpent always finds confidence in things other than God, but this is also a temptation for the church. What are the worldly things in which we are tempted to place our trust?

4. One of the lessons Esau teaches us is that we can't trust in outward signs for our salvation. Although Esau was born into a godly family and received the sign of circumcision, he was considered a reprobate in the eyes of God. Discuss how the lesson of Esau remains applicable to believers today. List and discuss some outward signs of apparent faithfulness in which we can mistakenly put our trust.

Chapter 5

AMAZING GRACE: JONAH

He was born into a Christian home and for the first six years of his life his mother faithfully taught him the Scriptures. Tragically, his mother died when he was six years old. When his father remarried, he was sent off to boarding school where he suffered under a cruel schoolmaster. His father was a mariner and at the age of eleven he began to accompany his father on his voyages. He continued a life at sea eventually working on a vessel engaged in the African slave trade. It was during this period that he led a truly profligate life. While at sea he faced many trials, including his own sinfulness and the violence of the sea. However, it was also during this time that he began to sense the convicting power of God and to recognize God's preserving grace. He eventually repented of his sin and embraced Jesus Christ as his Saviour. Later, as he reflected on God's grace, he wrote these famous words: 'Amazing Grace! How Sweet the Sound – That saved a wretch like me! I once was lost but now am found. Was blind but now I see.' After experiencing many 'dangers, toils and snares' John Newton was transformed by his encounter with God's amazing grace.[1]

The prophet Jonah experienced a similar journey of grace. Like Newton, Jonah was initially rebellious and resistant to God's work and, like Newton, it took peril on the seas to awaken him to the glories of God's grace.[2] Jonah teaches us about the extent of God's amazing grace which is ultimately revealed in Jesus Christ.

ENTERING INTO JONAH'S WORLD

Jonah prophesied during the eighth century B.C. At that time, Assyria was the most powerful nation in the Middle East. The capital of Assyria was the city of Nineveh. Nineveh was an impressive city with a large population. It was surrounded by high fortified walls. Assyria and its capital city of Nineveh dwarfed the tiny nation of Israel and its capital city of Jerusalem. The two nations were bitter rivals and Israel would have been very pleased to see Nineveh's downfall. To put it bluntly, Israel hated Nineveh and Jonah shared his nation's hatred of the Ninevites. Like Israel, Jonah wanted God to judge the Ninevites, but God had another plan. Much to Jonah's displeasure, God called him to go to the city of Nineveh and offer its inhabitants an opportunity to repent. As you might guess, Jonah was not thrilled about fulfilling his calling.

The prophecy of Jonah, much like that of Hosea, is conveyed through the life of the prophet himself. Essentially, Jonah became God's object lesson to convey his message of amazing grace. Jonah learned about grace by encountering it personally and by being forced to be an instrument of grace to the Ninevites.

THE RECALCITRANT PROPHET ENCOUNTERS PERSONAL GRACE

The first chapter of Jonah's prophecy opens with a command to Jonah to 'go'. God commissioned him, stating, 'Go to the great city of Nineveh and preach against it, because its wickedness has come up before me' (Jonah 1:20). What was Jonah's response to this call? He chose to ignore God's command and instead headed in the opposite direction: 'But Jonah ran away from the LORD and headed for Tarshish' (Jonah 1:3). Jonah did not want the Ninevites to experience God's grace, so instead of going to Nineveh, he headed for Tarshish. He could not have picked a more remote location. Tarshish was most likely located in what is now the nation of Spain. To the people of Jonah's day, Tarshish was the edge of the known world. It was in the exact opposite direction from Nineveh – Tarshish was west, Nineveh was east. Jonah boarded the ship to Tarshish in an effort to circumvent God's will, to prevent his extension of grace to the Ninevites.

On the voyage to Tarshish, Jonah continued to display his reluctance to extend God's grace to others. As the ship set sail, a massive storm arose and the pagan sailors became so afraid that they began to pray to their idols. What a great missionary opportunity for Jonah! He had an opportunity to alleviate the fear of the sailors by sharing with them the knowledge of the true God, but instead Jonah chose to go below deck and fall asleep. He didn't tell them about God. He didn't even intercede in prayer for them. Obviously, Jonah had no desire to extend God's grace to these pagan sailors.

God, however, was not going to let Jonah off the hook that easily. In his providence, God provided Jonah with other opportunities to evangelize the pagan sailors. First, God sent the pagan captain directly to Jonah: 'The captain went to him and said, "How can you sleep? Get up and call on your god! Maybe he will take notice of us, and we will not perish"' (Jonah 1:6). Here was another opportunity for Jonah to share the truth of the living God. Once again, however, he obstinately refused. Second, God sent the entire crew to Jonah. The crew cast lots to determine who was to blame for the storm and God made certain that the lot fell to Jonah. After the lot fell to him, the sailors approached Jonah and asked him to identify himself. He replied, 'I am a Hebrew and I worship the LORD, the God of heaven, who made the sea and the land' (Jonah 1:9). Finally, albeit reluctantly, Jonah shared the knowledge of the true God with the pagan sailors and amazingly they immediately believed![3] The sailors then asked Jonah what they should do in order to quell the storm. Jonah told them they had to throw him into the sea (Jonah 1:12). At first the sailors resisted this command, but they eventually obeyed and tossed the prophet overboard. The raging seas became calm, but Jonah's troubles were far from over. This was just the beginning!

The first chapter of Jonah's prophecy ends with these words: 'But the LORD provided a great fish to swallow Jonah, and Jonah was inside the fish three days and three nights' (Jonah 1:17). The storm was precarious enough, but now Jonah found himself in even greater peril. However, it was in the belly of the fish that Jonah began to learn about God's grace, for there he was totally helpless. He could no longer run away. He needed God's assistance and so he prayed to God for deliverance. God answered his prayers and three days later the fish vomited him onto dry land. God graciously delivered Jonah. Once Jonah was on dry land again, God repeated his original command: 'Then the word of the LORD came to Jonah a second time: "Go to the great city of Nineveh and proclaim to it the message I give you"' (Jonah 3:1). This time Jonah's reaction was markedly different. While he remained far from overjoyed with his task, he obeyed God: 'Jonah obeyed the word of the LORD and went to Nineveh' (Jonah 3:3).

Do you see how Jonah's perils at sea changed him? He was forced to recognize both God's sovereignty and his own need for grace. In the belly of the great fish, Jonah personally encountered God's grace. God used these experiences to prepare Jonah to become an instrument of grace to others, but Jonah still had a lot to learn.

THE RECALCITRANT PROPHET BECOMES AN INSTRUMENT OF GRACE

After Jonah's ordeal in the belly of the fish, he walked into the heart of the city of Nineveh to deliver God's message. However, when it came time for him to open his mouth, Jonah said the bare minimum that obedience required. His entire sermon is recorded for us in one verse: 'Forty more days and Nineveh will be overturned' (Jonah 3:4). That was it! Eight words in English, five in Hebrew! One can imagine Jonah hastily delivering his half-hearted sermon and then immediately exiting the city, hoping that no one would repent.

However, just like the sailors on the ship to Tarshish, the Ninevites responded favourably to Jonah's message (Jonah 3:5). This was an incredible act of God's grace! This wicked city repented! Jonah, however, was not impressed. Instead, he became angry, left the city, and built a shelter where he awaited God's reaction to the city of Nineveh (Jonah 4:1-5). Presumably, he was still hoping that Nineveh would be destroyed.

As Jonah sat sulking in his shelter, God continued to instruct him about grace. First, he provided a vine to shade Jonah from the scorching heat. This made Jonah happy momentarily, but the next day God sent a worm to kill the vine and Jonah quickly began to suffer from the heat. He then became very angry about the death of the vine. As he sat fuming in anger, God interrogated him: "'Do you have a right to be angry about the vine?" "I do", he said. "I am angry enough to die"' (Jonah 4:9). Next, God confronted Jonah with these words:

> But the LORD said, 'You have been concerned about this vine, though you did not tend it or make it grow. It sprang up overnight and died overnight. But Nineveh has more than a hundred and twenty thousand people who cannot tell their right hand from their left, and many cattle as well. Should I not be concerned about that great city?' (Jonah 4:10-11).

Do you see what God was teaching Jonah here? He was teaching Jonah a lesson about the nature of his sovereignty. God told Jonah that he made the vine, the worm and the Ninevites, therefore, he could do with each of them as he pleased. In essence, God was saying to Jonah, 'I will have mercy on whom I have mercy, and I will have compassion on whom I have compassion' (Exod. 33:19). In other words, God was informing Jonah that he may extend his grace to whomever he desires, even the Ninevites. God taught Jonah about the nature of his sovereign grace by forcing him to be an instrument of grace to the Ninevites.

Jonah learned about grace by encountering it personally and by being forced to be an instrument of grace to the Ninevites. However, Jonah had an even bigger role in explaining the grace of God. He was also used to point us to the One who is full of grace.

JESUS BRINGS GRACE TO ALL NATIONS

Jonah speaks of Jesus by foreshadowing and typifying the work of Jesus Christ in extending redemptive grace to all nations. Jonah is a type of Christ. Jesus confirms this by directly connecting Jonah to his own ministry in the Gospel of Matthew:

> Then some of the Pharisees and teachers of the law said to him, 'Teacher, we want to see a miraculous sign from you.' He answered, 'A wicked and adulterous generation asks for a miraculous sign! But none will be given it except the sign of the prophet Jonah. For as Jonah was three days and three nights in the belly of a huge fish, so the Son of Man will be three days and three nights in the heart of the earth. The men of Nineveh will stand up at the judgment with this generation and condemn it; for they repented at the preaching of Jonah, and now one greater than Jonah is here' (Matt. 12:39-41).

In this passage, Jesus draws two explicit parallels between his ministry and the ministry of Jonah. First, Jesus connects Jonah's three days in the belly of the fish to his own death and resurrection. Second, Jesus connects the preaching ministry of Jonah to his own by referring to how the people of Nineveh 'repented at the preaching of Jonah' (Matt. 12:41). By this connection, Jesus was informing the Pharisees and teachers of the law that they, like the people of Nineveh, needed to repent. In addition to these two explicit parallels, there is a third implied parallel between Jonah and Jesus which flows out of Matthew 12 and relates to the entire scope of the ministry of Christ. It is this implied parallel which most strongly reveals how Jonah speaks of Jesus.

One of the central lessons of Jonah is that God cares about all nations. At the time of Jonah, Israel believed that God only cared about them. Jonah was representative of this national belief and in that way he served as a microcosm for the entire nation. Jonah, like Israel as a whole, resisted the idea of God extending his grace to other nations. Jonah did not want to preach to the Ninevites because he did not want them to receive God's favour. However, God forced Jonah to be an instrument of his grace. Thus, God used Jonah to teach Israel that he cares about all nations. Remember God's question to Jonah at the end of the prophecy: 'But Nineveh has more than a hundred and twenty thousand people who cannot tell their right hand from their left, and many cattle as well. *Should I not be concerned about that great city?*' (Jonah 4:11, emphasis mine). Jonah is one of the clearest Old Testament examples that God's redemptive plan includes the extension of his grace to the Gentiles.

This theme from Jonah foreshadows the work of Jesus Christ. After Jonah spent three days in the great fish he came forth and preached to the Gentiles in Nineveh. After his resurrection, Jesus gave his disciples the following commission:

> Then Jesus came to them and said, 'All authority in heaven and on earth has been given to me. *Therefore go and make disciples of all nations,* baptizing them in the name of the Father and of the Son and of the Holy Spirit, and teaching them to obey everything I have commanded you. And surely I am with you always, to the very end of the age' (Matt. 28:18-20, emphasis mine).

Then, just before he ascended into heaven, he commanded his followers to carry the gospel to the ends of the earth (Acts 1:8). Jesus, like Jonah, is an instrument of grace to the Gentiles.

However, there is a vast difference between Jesus and Jonah. Jonah was a reluctant instrument of God's grace to the nations whereas Jesus was a willing servant. Jonah had an overly narrow view of God's redemptive plan. He did not want God to extend grace to 'those people'. He admits that he fled to Tarshish solely to prevent God's extension of his grace to the Ninevites: 'That is why I was so quick to flee to Tarshish. I knew that you are a gracious and compassionate God' (Jonah 4:2). Jesus, on the other hand, came to seek and save that which was lost (Luke 19:10). One of the marks of the ministry of Jesus was how he reached out to those long considered unworthy of God's grace including prostitutes, tax collectors, and Gentiles.

This difference between Jesus and Jonah raises profound questions for Christians today. Are we more like Jonah or Jesus? Are our churches reflective of the spirit of Jonah or the spirit of Jesus? Have we become reluctant and recalcitrant purveyors of grace? Are we like Old Testament Israel in our inwardness? Far too often the new covenant church, like Israel of old, has imposed unwarranted limits on the extent of God's redemptive plan. The prophecy of Jonah warns us that such behaviour can result in a loss of blessing for the people of God. Willem VanGemeren noted that Jonah's prophecy 'contains a strong warning to all the godly. The elect may miss the blessing of seeing God's grace extended outside the immediate covenant community because they impose limits on God.'[4] It is important for each Christian, and each congregation, to periodically reflect upon the question, 'Are we more like Jesus or Jonah when it comes to evangelism?'

JESUS IS THE ONE GREATER THAN JONAH

Clearly, based on Matthew 12:39-41, Jonah serves as a type of Jesus Christ. As discussed in the introduction to this book, one of the elements of biblical typology is 'escalation'. That is, the New Testament fulfilment of the type (the 'antitype') goes far beyond the original type from the Old Testament. This dynamic is apparent in the relationship between Jonah (the 'type') and Jesus (the 'antitype'). Jesus himself makes this very point in Matthew 12:41 when he states, 'Now one *greater* than Jonah is here', (emphasis mine). In what ways is Jesus greater than Jonah?

First, Jesus is greater than Jonah because Jesus sought to do the will of the Father while Jonah sought to do his own will. In the garden of Gethsemane, when Jesus confronted the horror of what lay before him, he told the Father, 'Yet not as I will, but as you will', (Matt. 26:39). Jesus laid down his life in obedience to the Father's will. He willingly went to the cross and the tomb. Jesus was a willing servant of the Father's will. Contrast that with Jonah's behaviour. When Jonah received God's command for his life, he ran the other way. God told Jonah to go to Nineveh and instead Jonah headed off for Tarshish. He unwillingly entered the belly of the fish. He had to be forced to go to Nineveh. Jonah did not want to see God's will fulfilled, but rather sought to have his own will fulfilled. In essence, Jonah said to God, 'Yet not as you will, but as I will.' Jonah was a reluctant and recalcitrant servant. Jesus is greater than Jonah because Jesus obeyed the will of his heavenly Father.

Second, Jesus is greater than Jonah because he displayed great mercy and compassion for the lost. Jesus lamented that Jerusalem was unrepentant: 'O Jerusalem, Jerusalem, you who kill the prophets and stone those sent to you, how often I have longed to gather your children together, as a hen gathers her chicks under her wings, but you were not willing!' (Luke 13:34, see also Luke 19:41). In 2 Peter 3:9, the apostle Peter describes Jesus as 'patient', 'not wanting anyone to perish', but rather desiring to see all his people 'come to repentance'. Jesus was filled with compassion for the lost: 'When he saw the crowds, he had compassion on them, because they were harassed and helpless, like sheep without a shepherd' (Matt. 9:36). Now contrast this with the spirit and attitude of Jonah. Jonah showed no compassion or mercy for the pagan sailors on the ship. He displayed no compassion for the lost in Nineveh, but rather displayed only disdain for them. Jonah was the exact opposite of Peter's description in 2 Peter 3:9. He was impatient. He wanted the Ninevites to perish. He did not want the Ninevites to come to repentance. Jonah did not lament over Nineveh's lack of repentance, rather he lamented because God desired to extend his grace to them. Jesus is greater than Jonah because he displays mercy and compassion for the lost.

Third, Jesus is greater than Jonah because he is the greatest of all the prophets. In Deuteronomy 18:18-19 God promised Israel that he would one day send a great prophet like Moses: 'I will raise up for them a prophet like you from among their brothers; I will put my words in his mouth, and he will tell them everything I command him. If anyone does not listen to my words that the prophet speaks in my name, I myself will call him to account.' The New Testament verifies that Jesus is the prophet promised by God in Deuteronomy 18 (see Acts 3:22 and 7:37). When Jesus stood before the Pharisees and teachers of the law he told them that 'one greater than Jonah is here'. He was telling them that the greatest prophet had come. He was telling them that if they did not listen to his words, then God would call them to account. The stinging indictment Jesus laid against the Pharisees and teachers of the law in Matthew 12:39-41 was the fact that the lesser prophet Jonah went to the Ninevites and they repented, but now the greatest prophet was before them and they would not heed his message. When we compare the prophetic ministry of Jonah and Jesus, Jonah is truly the 'minor' prophet. Jesus is greater than Jonah because he is the greatest of all the prophets.

Fourth, Jesus is greater than Jonah because he is the very source of God's grace. Jesus was not only a messenger and instrument of God's grace, but he was its source as well. The apostle John describes Jesus as being 'full of grace and truth' (John 1:14), and states that while the law came through Moses, 'grace and truth came through Jesus Christ' (John 1:17). The apostle Paul also confirms that Jesus is the source of grace:

For he chose us in him before the creation of the world to be holy and blameless in his sight. In love he predestined us to be adopted as his sons through Jesus Christ, in accordance with his pleasure and will — *to the praise of his glorious grace, which he has freely given us in the One he loves* (Eph. 1:4-6, emphasis mine).

To further emphasize this point, Paul often connected grace to the person of Jesus Christ at the beginning and end of his letters to the churches. For example, at the beginning of his first letter to the Corinthians, Paul greeted them by stating, 'Grace and peace to you from God our Father and the Lord Jesus Christ' (1 Cor.

1:3).[5] In a similar manner, Paul ended his letter to the Romans with these words, 'The grace of our Lord Jesus Christ be with you' (Rom. 16:20)[6] Jesus is the very embodiment of grace. This is something Jonah could never be.

Fifth, Jesus is greater than Jonah because Christ literally, rather than figuratively, rose from the dead. Whereas Jonah spent three days in the belly of the great fish, Jesus spent three days in the grave (Matt. 12:40). Although Jonah's suffering is figuratively connected to Christ's suffering, there really is no comparison when one considers the difference in the magnitude of suffering experienced by them and what their respective sufferings accomplished. O. Palmer Robertson notes the vast difference between the sufferings and accomplishments of Jonah and Christ:

> All praise to Jesus Christ the suffering servant of the Lord! He endured things worse than Jonah. Hell itself was his cup to drink, not merely a mouthful of salt water. The Lord pursued Jonah to the point of death for the sake of the salvation of many, but he pursued Christ to the fact of hell to save numberless sinners throughout the history of the world.[7]

Furthermore, while Jonah was in the belly of the fish due to his own sinfulness, Jesus entered the grave for our sins. Jonah's figurative resurrection is only indirectly related to the conversion of the Ninevites, but Jesus' resurrection is directly related to the justification of believers: 'He was delivered over to death for our sins and was raised to life for our justification' (Rom. 4:25).

The type of Jonah is eclipsed by the glory of the antitype Jesus. Jesus is greater than Jonah because he is the very source of grace. He is full of grace.

Amazing Grace
It is true that the book of Jonah teaches us the extent to which God will go to show grace to those he loves, but think about how much more this is displayed in the sending of Jesus. 'For God so

loved the world that he gave his one and only Son, that whoever believes in him shall not perish but have eternal life' (John 3:16). Do you understand the fulness of God's amazing grace? Jonah only foreshadows it. He only scratches the surface. In Jesus we see the fulness of God's amazing grace and love: 'But God demonstrates his own love for us in this: While we were still sinners, Christ died for us' (Rom. 5:8). It is an amazing thing that Jesus came to save sinners like us.

John Newton, the author of the hymn 'Amazing Grace', recognized that the most amazing thing about God's grace was that it came to him: 'If I ever reach heaven I expect to find three wonders there: first, to meet some I had not thought to see there; second, to miss some I had thought to meet there; and third, and the greatest wonder of all, to find myself there.'[8] That's the amazing thing about grace – it can even save wretches like Newton, like the Ninevites, like Jonah, and like you and me!

What is the proper response to God's amazing grace? We should be like the king of the Ninevites who stated: '…Let everyone call urgently on God. Let them give up their evil ways and their violence. Who knows? God may yet relent and with compassion turn from his fierce anger so that we will not perish' (Jonah 3:8-10). Our response should be to believe in the one who is greater than Jonah! That's how Jonah speaks of Jesus.

Questions for Discussion

1. It is very easy to be critical of Jonah regarding his resistance to go and share the gospel with the Ninevites. However, before we rush to judgement it is important for us to remember that Christ commands us to share the gospel with those around us. Have you, like Jonah, failed to pray for the conversions of others? Have you, like Jonah, failed to take advantage of opportunities to share the gospel with the lost? Discuss some concrete examples of how you are like Jonah when it comes to evangelism and then discuss ways to avoid these mistakes.

2. Jonah did not like the Ninevites because they were Israel's enemy and they were foreigners. Simply put, the Ninevites

were different. Often believers find themselves in churches which have homogeneous populations. This tendency often reduces the church's effectiveness in spreading the gospel. Discuss whether this dynamic is at work in your congregation. Discuss how this dynamic can create obstacles to effective evangelism. Finally, discuss how you and your congregation can endeavour to overcome these obstacles.

3. Jonah had to experience grace personally before he was able to extend it to others. Discuss and share your own personal journey of grace. Consider how you first heard the gospel and why your personal journey of grace should motivate your desire to share the gospel with others.

4. Recall and discuss the five ways in which Jesus is greater than Jonah. Discuss what this contrast teaches us about the nature and work of Jesus Christ. Also discuss how this contrast should encourage us in our evangelism.

Chapter 6

WHAT THE LORD REQUIRES: MICAH

Would God ask you to do something that you are unable to do? Would God require something of you which you are unable to provide? Questions such as these led to an intense debate in the early church. On one side of the debate was Saint Augustine (A.D. 354-430) who recorded in his *Confessions* the following prayer to God: 'Grant what Thou commandest, and command what Thou dost desire.' Do you see what Augustine was requesting in his prayer? He was asking God to grant him the ability to do what God commanded of him. Augustine believed that he could not meet God's standards in his own power. He believed that God does require something of us which we are unable to provide in ourselves.

On the other side of the debate was a British monk named Pelagius. Augustine's prayer enraged Pelagius because he could not accept that God would demand something of his creatures which they were unable to render to him. He believed that all men were, by nature, capable of doing what the Lord requires of them without supernatural assistance from God. Augustine's view eventually prevailed and in A.D. 431, at the Council at Ephesus, the church condemned the teaching of Pelagius. At that council, the church collectively stated that God does require a standard of us which we are unable to satisfy in our own power.

The book of Micah deals with a similar issue. Micah informs the people of Israel and Judah that God demands righteousness from them. He demands it of the leaders of the people and of every citizen in his kingdom. Micah declares to Israel and Judah what the Lord requires of them. The only problem is – they can't do it.

ENTERING INTO MICAH'S WORLD

Micah prophesied in the latter part of the eighth-century B.C. His prophetic ministry lasted more than thirty years. During his ministry he witnessed the fall of Israel to Assyria in 722 B.C. and attacks on Judah by the armies of Sennacherib (2 Kings 18:13-16). Foreign invasions, however, were not Israel and Judah's biggest problems. Their main problems were domestic.

The social climate of Micah's time was dire. The people of God were oppressing the poor (2:1-3), perverting justice through corrupt courts (3:1-3), and engaging in fraudulent commercial practices (6:10-11). The wickedness was particularly acute in the offices of leadership. The three offices of prophet, priest and king were infested with corruption. The land was filled with false prophets (3:5-7), the priests were greedy (3:11), and the rulers despised justice (3:9). Micah 3:11 aptly summarizes the spiritual condition of the leadership during Micah's ministry: 'Her leaders judge for a bribe, her priests teach for a price, and her prophets tell fortunes for money.' At the time of Micah's ministry, the people and their leaders were both practicing unrighteousness. It is into this setting that God sends Micah.

THE CASE AGAINST ISRAEL AND JUDAH

Micah's job is similar to that of a prosecuting attorney. God has sent him to register his complaint against Israel and Judah, to prosecute his covenant lawsuit. This courtroom motif is vividly displayed in the sixth chapter of Micah. It commences in Micah 6:1-2 where God calls his court to order: 'Stand up, plead your case before the mountains; let the hills hear what you have to say. Hear, O mountains, the LORD's accusation; listen, you everlasting foundations of the earth. For the LORD has a case against his people; he is lodging a charge against Israel.' God is about to charge his people and he calls forth two great witnesses to hear the charges – the mountains and the foundations of the earth.[1] Next, in verses 3-5, God begins to make his case against his people:

> My people, what have I done to you? How have I burdened you? Answer me. I brought you up out of Egypt and redeemed you from the land of slavery. I sent Moses to lead you, also Aaron and Miriam. My people, remember what Balak king of Moab counseled and what Balaam son of Beor answered. Remember your journey from Shittim to Gilgal, that you may know the righteous acts of the LORD.

Do you see what God was charging them with here? He was charging them with forgetting his mighty acts in history, forgetting his redemptive grace. He even invoked the covenant at Sinai against them in verse 4 by echoing the words of Exodus 20:2: 'I am the LORD your God, who brought you out of Egypt, out of the land of slavery.' God was accusing Israel and Judah of forgetting his redemptive grace, of forgetting his covenant. The evidence that they had forgotten God's covenant was their national and personal unrighteousness. God delivered Israel out of bondage in

Egypt so that they would be a holy nation, but they had become the exact opposite.

In verses 6-7 we see the response of the people given through an individual spokesman, perhaps the prophet himself:

> With what shall I come before the LORD and bow down before the exalted God? Shall I come before him with burnt offerings, with calves a year old? Will the LORD be pleased with thousands of rams, with ten thousand rivers of oil? Shall I offer my firstborn for my transgression, the fruit of my body for the sin of my soul?

This response demonstrates how far Israel and Judah had fallen spiritually. They were not sure what would please God, but their best guess was that it involved paying him off through empty ritual. John Calvin aptly captured the attitude of the people in his comments on this passage: 'Hence they wish to discharge their duty towards God as a matter of necessity; but at the same time seek some fictitious modes of reconciliation, as though it were enough to flatter God, as though he could be pacified like a child with some frivolous trifles.'[2] Their view of God had fallen so low that they were treating him like an idol which could be satiated by frivolous sacrifices.

In verse 8, God clarifies the situation by telling Israel and Judah exactly what he requires of them: 'He has showed you, O man, what is good. And what does the LORD require of you? To act justly and to love mercy and to walk humbly with your God.' Essentially God told them, 'I don't want your sacrifices, I want your obedience!' God demanded righteousness from his people. He demanded that they act justly, love mercy and walk humbly with him. The problem for Israel and Judah was that they were not doing these things. Their leaders – prophets, priests and kings – were morally bankrupt. They hated justice and mercy. They were not walking humbly with their God. The corruption, however, extended far beyond the leadership. Remember, every citizen of Israel and Judah was brought before God's court in Micah 6 and each of them was found guilty as charged!

Micah informs us that the people of God had two problems. First, they lacked righteous leadership. Second, they lacked personal righteousness. These two problems were exacerbated by the fact that the people were unable to do what the Lord required of them in their own power. In order to satisfy God's righteous requirement, the people had to look outside themselves for a deliverer. They had to turn their eyes to the future hope of a Messiah. They had to turn their eyes to Jesus.

JESUS IS THE RIGHTEOUS LEADER

As noted in the beginning of this chapter, one of the major problems facing the people of Israel and Judah was that they lacked righteous leaders. The offices of prophet, priest and king were rife with corruption. Due to the unrighteousness of their leadership, Micah prophesied that Israel and Judah would soon enter into bondage. They would once again become slaves to a foreign nation like they had been in Egypt. However, the prophecy of Micah also contains a message of great hope. It contains the promise of a coming righteous leader. Micah promises that God will send the people a righteous shepherd-king.

In the second chapter of Micah's prophecy he describes the coming of a great leader who will liberate the people of Israel. Micah describes this future leader as a shepherd who 'breaks open the way' for his sheep:

> I will surely gather all of you, O Jacob; I will surely bring together the remnant of Israel. I will bring them together like sheep in a pen, like a flock in its pasture; the place will throng with people. One who breaks open the way will go up before them; they will break through the gate and go out. Their king will pass through before them, the LORD at their head (Micah 2:12-13).

Micah promises that Israel will one day have a righteous leader, a great shepherd, who will lead them out of bondage.

In the New Testament Jesus identifies himself as the 'good shepherd' (John 10:11). The adjective 'good' indicates that Jesus is a noble and worthy shepherd. It implies that he cares for his sheep. Jesus expressed his concern and love for his sheep by laying down his life for them (John 10:11). This sacrificial and righteous act of the good shepherd broke open the way for the redemption of his sheep. The cross marked the commencement of the new exodus.[3] Jesus came to deliver his sheep out of bondage to Satan, sin and death. Jesus liberates the lost sheep of Israel, but he also 'breaks open the way' for the Gentiles as well: 'I have other sheep that are not of this sheep pen. I must bring them also. They too will listen to my voice, and there shall be one flock and one shepherd' (John 10:16). Jesus is the shepherd who liberates his people, both Jew and Gentile, and makes them into one flock. Jesus is the great shepherd of the sheep predicted by Micah (Heb. 13:20).

Furthermore, Micah informs us that this future leader will not only be a shepherd, but he will also be a king. This connection is made in two places in Micah's prophecy. First, it occurs in the passage we just examined. For example, in Micah 2:13 the future leader is spoken of as both a shepherd and a king. In the first part of verse 13, Micah employs the shepherd metaphor by depicting the people as sheep being led out of the gate by the shepherd, the 'one who breaks open the way': 'One who breaks open the way will go up before them; they will break through the gate and go out.' In the second part of verse 13, Micah speaks of the shepherd as a king: 'Their king will pass through before them, the LORD at their head.' The second place Micah makes this connection is in Micah 5:1-5:

> Marshal your troops, O city of troops, for a siege is laid against us. They will strike *Israel's ruler* on the cheek with a rod. 'But you, Bethlehem Ephrathah, though you are small among the clans of Judah, out of you will come for me one *who will be ruler over Israel*, whose origins are from of old, from ancient times.' Therefore Israel will be abandoned until the time when she who is in labor gives birth and the rest of his brothers return to join the Israel-

ites. He will *stand and shepherd his flock* in the strength of the LORD, in the majesty of the name of the LORD his God. And they will live securely, for then his greatness will reach to the ends of the earth. And he will be their peace (emphasis mine).

Micah promises Israel and Judah that they will one day be ruled by a righteous king. This king will come from Bethlehem, the hometown of King David. He will be a divine and eternal king ('whose origins are from of old, from ancient times'). He will also be human ('when she who is in labor gives birth').[4] He will impact the entire world ('his greatness will reach to the ends of the earth'). He will bring peace to his people ('And he will be their peace'). What a king! Only Jesus can match this description provided by Micah. Jesus is the great king spoken of by the prophet.

This interpretation is confirmed by the Gospel of Matthew. Nearly seven hundred years after Micah's prophecy, King Herod learned that a king had been born, a king who threatened his throne. Herod wanted to locate this king so he could destroy him. Therefore, he called together the chief priests and the teachers of the law and asked them where this king would be born. Matthew records their reply to Herod:

'In Bethlehem in Judea', they replied, 'for this is what the prophet has written: "But you, Bethlehem, in the land of Judah, are by no means least among the rulers of Judah; for out of you will come a ruler who will be the shepherd of my people Israel"' (Matt. 2:5-6).

The righteous ruler promised by Micah is the Lord Jesus Christ!

In Micah's day, Israel and Judah were suffering because they had corrupt leaders. Micah told them that one day a righteous leader would come. He promised them a great shepherd and a great king. These two promises were fulfilled in Jesus Christ.

The fact that Jesus is our great shepherd and our great king should provide us with great comfort for we too suffer from a lack of righteous leadership. We know that Proverbs tells us that 'Righteousness exalts a nation, but sin is a disgrace to any people' (Prov. 14:34). Our headlines are filled with political and religious scandals. Both political and religious leaders too often refer to evil as good. This can lead Christians to great despair and frustration. While we should pray for our leaders and seek righteous people to rule over us both in the civil and ecclesiastical realms, we must always remember that our hope for righteous leadership can only be satisfied by looking to Jesus Christ. In this way we are very much like the people of God at Micah's time. They were waiting for the ruler to come; we are waiting for him to come again. For we know that when he comes again, 'He will judge the world in righteousness and the peoples with equity' (Ps. 98:9).

JESUS IS OUR RIGHTEOUSNESS

While Israel and Judah's lack of righteous leadership was a problem, it was not their biggest problem. They had a much deeper and more personal problem. The people could not keep God's standard of righteousness. As you will recall, God told the people what he required of them: 'To act justly and to love mercy and to walk humbly with your God' (Micah 6:8). At first glance, this three-fold requirement may not have seemed so overwhelming to them. After all, there are only three commands, right? They were probably thinking that this simple triad was much less burdensome than the Ten Commandments and all those miscellaneous laws in Leviticus, Numbers and Deuteronomy. Perhaps they were thinking that God's standards were changing, that he was requiring less of them. If they were thinking in this fashion, then they were gravely mistaken.

I contend that the three-fold standard expressed in Micah 6:8 is simply a shorthand way of referring to the eternal standard of God's moral law as summarized in the Ten Commandments. Perhaps you are thinking that I am stretching it a bit. Perhaps you are asking yourself, 'Is Micah 6:8 really a reference to the Ten Commandments?' Well let's consider the substance of this triad for a few moments.

First, acting justly here means more than cleaning up corrupt courts. It is a call to order one's entire life according to the revealed will of God. It means living in compliance with God's standards of righteousness, particularly with regards to the treatment of others. As Willem VanGemeren noted, 'Justice, as it pertains to human beings, is that quality of integrity by which one deals with people in accordance with God's standard.'[5] In Micah 6:8, God was calling on Israel and Judah to act justly in their relationship with their neighbours.

Second, is the command to love mercy. The word translated as 'mercy' here is the Hebrew word *hesed* which means expressing faithfulness in a covenant relationship. God expressed his mercy to the Israelites in the context of his covenant relationship with them. Here he calls on them to do the same to their neighbours. They are to show mercy to their neighbours.

Third, the call to walk humbly with God has a deeper meaning than simply showing God a modicum of respect. It is primarily a call to carefully and circumspectly walk with God, to walk with him as Enoch walked with him (Gen. 5:24). Therefore, to walk humbly with God is particularly related to the people's spiritual service to God. Israel was called to be a nation of priests. They were called to approach the living God and those who approach God must honour him (Lev. 10:3).

As you can see, this three-fold standard is incredibly broad in its scope. It called for the people of Israel and Judah to do two things: to love their neighbours and to love their God. Are not these two requirements at the heart of the Ten Commandments? For example, the first two (to act justly and love mercy) are very similar to the substance contained in the last five commandments or the so-called 'second table' of the law. The final element (walk humbly with your God) is similar in substance to the first four commandments or the 'first table' of the law.

Others have noticed this connection between Micah 6:8 and the Ten Commandments.

For example, John Calvin stated the following in his commentary on Micah 6:8: 'It is evident that, in the two first particulars, he refers to the second table of the Law, that is, to do justice and to love mercy.'[6] The renowned Old Testament scholar C.F. Keil agreed with Calvin, noting that to act justly and love mercy embraced 'all the commandments of the second table'. Matthew Henry contended that the third part of the triad (to walk humbly with your God) '...includes all the duties of the first table, as the two former include all the duties of the second table'.[7] Micah 6:8 summarizes God's eternal standard of righteousness, his moral law. The problem for the people of Israel and Judah was that they could not meet this standard of righteousness. As stated earlier, when God brought his case against the people in Micah 6, they were guilty as charged. They were unable to do what God commanded of them.

It is important to remember that Micah 6:8 is not merely some Old Testament matter. Jesus brought the very same case against Israel during his earthly ministry. In Matthew 23:23, Jesus confronted the Pharisees. Notice the familiarity of the charge he brings against them: 'Woe to you, teachers of the law and Pharisees, you hypocrites! You give a tenth of your spices – mint, dill and cummin. But you have neglected the more important matters of the law – *justice, mercy and faithfulness.* You should have practised the latter, without neglecting the former' (Matt. 23:23, emphasis mine). Doesn't the triad 'justice, mercy and faithfulness' sound very much like Micah 6:8? As William Hendriksen noted, 'As to the triad "justice, mercy and faithfulness" it would be difficult to find a better commentary than the one offered by Micah 6:8.'[8] Jesus was holding the Pharisees to the same eternal standard of righteousness.

Another connection between Micah 6:8 and the New Testament can be seen in the encounter between Jesus and the rich young ruler. Note the question that the rich young ruler asks of Jesus: 'As Jesus started on his way, a man ran up to him and fell on his knees before him. "Good teacher," he asked, "what must I do to inherit eternal life?"' (Mark 10:17).[9] Isn't this the very same question that Israel and Judah asked of God in Micah 6? They too wanted to know what God required of them. Jesus gives a similar answer to the rich young ruler. He says to keep the law: 'You know the commandments: "Do not murder, do not commit adultery, do not steal, do not give false testimony, do not defraud, honor your father and mother.'" (Mark 10:19). Jesus is saying is that there is only one standard of righteousness and that is God's holy law.

God's standard of righteousness never changes. He commanded that Israel and Judah keep his law. The problem was they were failing to keep it. They were acting unjustly, they were not merciful, and they were not walking humbly with God. Their problem was they could not fulfil God's righteous standard on their own. Israel and Judah could not fulfil it, the Pharisees and teachers of the law could not fulfil it, the rich young ruler could not fulfil it, and you cannot fulfil it either. Do you always act justly? Do you always love mercy? Do you always walk humbly with God? Do you always keep the commandments? The problem addressed by Micah is not an ancient one; it is our problem. The good news is that Jesus Christ did fulfil God's righteous standard on behalf of his people!

The New Testament tells us that Jesus was born under the law (Gal. 4:4) and that he came, not to abolish the law, but to fulfil it (Matt. 5:17).[9] Paul tells us that through the obedience of Christ we are made righteous (Rom. 5:19). Through Jesus, we become the righteousness of God: 'God made him who had no sin to be sin for us, so that in him we might become the righteousness of God' (2 Cor. 5:21). Jesus Christ is the great Law-Keeper. He not only delivers you out of bondage to sin, but he also makes you righteous. He not only went to the cross for you, but he lived Micah 6:8 for you. He kept the law for you. He acted justly. He loved mercy. He humbled himself and walked faithfully with the Father. Jesus is our righteousness!

GOD'S RIGHTEOUS REQUIREMENT IS FULFILLED
God does ask of us something that we are unable to do in our own power. He demands perfection. Thankfully, he also grants us perfection in Jesus Christ. Jesus is the answer to Augustine's prayer, 'Grant what Thou commandest, and command what Thou dost desire.' In Jesus, God granted to us what he commanded of us. Through our union with Christ we are enabled to fulfil the

righteous requirements of the law. The apostle Paul makes this very point in Romans 8:3-4:

> For what the law was powerless to do in that it was weakened by the sinful nature, God did by sending his own Son in the likeness of sinful man to be a sin offering. And so he condemned sin in sinful man, in order that the righteous requirements of the law might be fully met in us, who do not live according to the sinful nature but according to the Spirit.

Robert Haldane commented on these verses as follows: 'They who are saved by mercy have that very righteousness that the law demands. In Christ they have paid the penalty of their disobedience, and in Christ they have yielded obedience to every precept of the law.'[10] In other words, through our union with Jesus Christ, and by the power of the sanctifying work of the Holy Spirit, we too can act justly, love mercy and walk humbly with our God. That's how Micah speaks of Jesus!

QUESTIONS FOR DISCUSSION

1. Micah's prophecy describes a society rife with corruption at all levels of government, in the church and in the marketplace. Attempt to identify modern day parallels to this aspect of Micah's prophecy. Discuss how Christians should react to corruption in these areas of life.

2. Consider again this quotation from John Calvin in which he captures the attitude of the church during Micah's time: 'Hence they wish to discharge their duty towards God as a matter of necessity; but at the same time seek some fictitious modes of reconciliation, as though it were enough to flatter God, as though he could be pacified like a child with some frivolous trifles.'[11] Discuss how we fall into the same sins as individual Christians and as Christian communities.

3. Read the following definition of sanctification as expressed in the Westminster Confession of Faith:

> They, who are once effectually called, and regenerated, having a new heart, and a new spirit created in them, are further sanctified, really and personally, through the virtue of Christ's death and resurrection, by his Word and Spirit dwelling in them: the dominion of the whole body of sin is destroyed, and the several lusts thereof are more and more weakened and mortified; and they more and more quickened and strengthened in all saving graces, to the practice of true holiness, without which no man shall see the Lord (Westminster Confession of Faith 13:1).

Discuss how this definition relates to Augustine's prayer ('Grant what Thou commandest, and command what Thou dost desire') and to Romans 8:3-4.

4. One of the main points of this chapter is that Christ is our righteousness. Discuss how the following texts relate to this principle: Romans 3:22-28; 4:5-8; 5:17-19; 1 Corinthians 1:30-31; 2 Corinthians 5:19-21; Ephesians 1:7 and Titus 3:5-7.

Chapter 7

NIGHT FALLS ON THE DAY OF GRACE: NAHUM

Jonathan Edwards is regarded by many as the greatest theologian America ever produced. He studied Latin at the age of six, entered Yale at the age of thirteen and graduated at fifteen. He was ordained as a minister at nineteen, taught at Yale when he was twenty and later became the president of Princeton. Although Jonathan Edwards had many impressive accomplishments during his life, he is probably best known for what he did on Sunday morning July 8, 1741. On that day, Edwards entered the pulpit of a church in Enfield, Connecticut, opened his Bible to Deuteronomy 32:35 and preached his famous sermon, 'Sinners in the Hands of an Angry God'.

In that sermon, Edwards warned the unconverted that they were ever so close to experiencing God's judgement and wrath. He declared, 'The bow of God's wrath is bent, and the arrow made ready on the string, and justice bends the arrow at your heart, and strains the bow, and it is nothing but the mere pleasure of God, and that of an angry God, without any promise or obligation at all, that keeps the arrow one moment from being made drunk with your blood.'[1] The point of Edwards' sermon was that judgement is coming, that God's grace has limits, that the time is short, and that night is about to fall on the day of grace. The prophet Nahum came with a similar message for the people of Nineveh. Nahum reminds us that the time of God's grace is limited. However, as we shall also see, this message of judgement provides great comfort for God's people.

ENTERING INTO NAHUM'S WORLD

Nahum prophesied during the mid to late seventh century B.C. At that time, Assyria was the world's leading empire and its capital city was Nineveh. As you will recall from previous chapters, Assyria had conquered the northern ten tribes of Israel in the eighth century B.C. and deported the people. As Nahum began his prophetic ministry, ten of the twelve tribes were gone and Judah was under constant threat from Assyria. It was into this setting that God sent Nahum. Nahum's message is one of impending judgement against Assyria, particularly against the city of Nineveh.

Perhaps you are saying to yourself at this point, 'Wait a minute, I thought Jonah preached to Nineveh and the city repented? Why are they now facing judgement?' It is true that Jonah went to Nineveh and the city repented in the eighth century B.C. Jesus himself affirmed the validity of the repentance offered by this first generation of Ninevites (Matt. 12:41). However, the descendants of this generation proved to be unfaithful to God. Instead of continuing to honour the God of Israel, they chose rather to invade and conquer Israel in the latter part of that very same century. By the time Nahum came on the scene, Nineveh's wickedness had grown so great that Nahum described the city in the following manner: 'Woe to the city of blood, full of lies, full of plunder, never without victims!' (Nahum 3:1). Given these facts, it is perhaps best to understand Nahum's prophecy as a sequel to Jonah's prophecy. Jonah told of God's grace, but God's grace has limits and Nahum explains what happens when God's grace reaches those limits.

In the prophecy of Nahum we are witnessing the twilight of the Assyrian Empire. Night is falling on the day of grace. The bow of God's wrath is drawn and ready. Nahum declares to Nineveh and the people of God that he is coming as a judge, a warrior and a deliverer.

The Prophet's Message: God is a Judge, Warrior and Deliverer

Nahum's message is unambiguous. He does not mince words. In the opening verses, the prophet gets right to the point. He tells Nineveh that God is angry and he's coming to judge. Nahum warns Nineveh that God is coming to redress the grievances of his people. He is coming to set things right. In the second verse of his prophecy, Nahum declares that the Lord is 'jealous', 'avenging' and 'filled with wrath' (Nahum 1:2). God once came to Nineveh full of grace, but now he is coming to execute his justice. Nahum tells Nineveh that God will not leave the 'guilty unpunished' (Nahum 1:3). In other words, Nahum is alerting Nineveh that its days are numbered. God is coming as a judge.

Nahum also informs Nineveh that God is not only coming to judge them, but also to make war against them. He is coming to utterly vanquish his enemies. The book of Nahum contains some of the most eloquent, beautiful and sophisticated poetry of the Old Testament. However, it is also horrific poetry. It is war poetry. In Nahum 1:3 God the warrior is described as a great storm ('His way is in the whirlwind and the storm') and as the great cloud rider ('and clouds are the dust of his feet.')[2] The divine warrior comes to make war as an awesome storm. He comes riding the clouds like massive cosmic stallions. Then in Nahum 1:4 the prophet describes the result of God's war making. He tells them that the seas and rivers will dry up and that the fruitful lands of Bashan, Carmel and Lebanon will become desolate. When God comes as a warrior, 'The mountains quake before him and the hills melt away.

The earth trembles at his presence, the world and all who live in it' (Nahum 1:5). After describing the awesome war-making power of God, Nahum posits two rhetorical questions: 'Who can withstand his indignation? Who can endure his fierce anger?' (Nahum 1:6). Nahum tells the Ninevites that they will not survive the wrath of his coming. When God mounts the clouds, when night falls on the day of grace, God's victory will be utter victory. His enemies will not survive when God comes to make war.

Not all of Nahum's prophecy is devoid of comfort, however. Nahum declared to Nineveh that God was coming to judge them and make war against them, but then in verse 7 the prophet turns from Nineveh to speak words of comfort to the people of God. Nahum reminds God's people that: 'The LORD is good, a refuge in times of trouble. He cares for those who trust in him.' Here we see that the wrath of God is not for those who trust in him, but only for his foes. Those who trust in God will see that the Lord is good and he will be a refuge for them. Nahum is telling Judah that God's judgement on Nineveh will result in their deliverance. As Willem VanGemeren put it, 'Every judgment on the wicked confirms his promise of protection given to all who suffer, trusting and waiting the justice of God.'[3] Nahum told Judah that they would find refuge in the coming storm, but Nineveh would come to a dreadful end. God promised to be a deliverer of his people.

God promised that he would come as a judge, warrior and deliverer. He promised that he would destroy Nineveh and liberate Judah. God kept his promise and the prophecy of Nahum was fulfilled in 612 B.C. when God sent the Babylonians to besiege Nineveh. The Babylonians surrounded the city of Nineveh for over two months. They eventually breached the walls and destroyed the city. Nineveh was brought to an abrupt end.

Given its emphasis on the destruction of Nineveh, one of the questions raised by the prophecy of Nahum is, 'What are we to make of it today?' Many view Nahum as a book which has no relevance for New Testament believers. They say it is indicative of an Old Testament ethic which has passed away with the coming of Jesus. After all, isn't the ministry of Jesus about peace and love rather than judgement and wrath? So where does this leave

Nahum? Is this just an Old Testament story about an Old Testament God? Is God still a judge, warrior and deliverer? Are there still limits to God's grace? To answer these questions we must turn our eyes to Jesus.

JESUS IS A JUDGE

Nahum prophesied that God was coming to judge the nation of Assyria. The judgement of Assyria serves as a type of the final judgement which God will bring upon all rebellious nations on the last great day. Who will execute God's judgement on that day? The Bible, both Old and New Testaments, consistently tells us that Jesus will judge the nations. For example, in the Old Testament, Psalm 110 places the judgement of the nations firmly in the purview of the Son of God stating, 'He will judge the nations, heaping up the dead and crushing the rulers of the whole earth' (Psalm 110:6). The New Testament reaffirms that it is specifically Jesus who serves as judge: 'Moreover, the Father judges no one, but has entrusted all judgment to the Son' (John 5:22). The Bible teaches us that Jesus is a judge.

There is another aspect of judgement set forth in Nahum which finds a parallel in the work of Jesus Christ. Jesus is not only a judge, but he also follows the same pattern of judgement described in Nahum. In the book of Nahum, the prophet informs Nineveh that God is not rash in his judgement and wrath, but rather that he is 'slow to anger' (Nahum 1:3). Nahum was informing Nineveh that God is a just and merciful God who delays his judgement in order to grant people ample time to repent. However, Nahum makes it equally clear that just because God has delayed judgement does not mean it will not come. Nahum makes this point by declaring to Nineveh, 'the Lord will not leave the guilty unpunished' (Nahum 1:3). Essentially, Nahum was saying that there is a day of grace, but there is also a day of judgement. Nahum came to tell Nineveh that night had fallen on their day of grace. He emphasized this point by selectively quoting from Exodus 34:6-7 in Nahum 1:3. Note some of the words Nahum chose to exclude from his quotation of Exodus (the noteworthy excluded words appear in bold print):

And he passed in front of Moses, proclaiming, 'The LORD, the LORD, **the compassionate and gracious God**, slow to anger, **abounding in love and faithfulness, maintaining love to thousands, and forgiving wickedness, rebellion and sin.** Yet he does not leave the guilty unpunished; he punishes the children and their children for the sin of the fathers to the third and fourth generation.' (Exod. 34:6-7)

'The LORD is slow to anger and great in power; the LORD will not leave the guilty unpunished. His way is in the whirlwind and the storm, and clouds are the dust of his feet.' (Nahum 1:3)

Nahum chose to exclude many of the words which describe God's grace. He left out the part about God being a 'compassionate and gracious God', a God who is 'abounding in love and faithfulness, maintaining love to thousands, and forgiving wickedness, rebellion and sin'. Why did the prophet leave these words out? It was because Nineveh had exhausted the day of grace. Night had fallen on the day of grace for Nineveh.

A similar dynamic is displayed in the New Testament in the work of Jesus Christ.

Jesus is slow to anger, but he will by no means leave the guilty unpunished. Jesus leaves ample time for people to repent, but he has also set a day for judgement. Paul made this very point in his sermon on Mars Hill:

In the past God overlooked such ignorance, but now he commands all people everywhere to repent. For he has set a day when he will judge the world with justice by the man he has appointed. He has given proof of this to all men by raising him from the dead (Acts 17:30-31).

Paul proclaimed that the Day of Judgement is fixed. The clock is ticking. There are limits to God's grace! Jesus will by no means leave the guilty unpunished. He is the man appointed as the judge of the world and he is coming to judge!

Nahum's message is relevant for us today because Jesus is coming to judge and the time for repentance is growing short. Nineveh did not heed God's warning and their time ran out. They mistook God's slowness to anger as a lack of resolve. Because God had delayed his judgement the Ninevites assumed he would not come in judgement. In our day, many people are making the very same mistake. They are living lives they know are wrong, but God's judgement has not yet fallen on them so they continue to indulge upon God's slowness to anger, mistaking it for a lack of resolve. They begin to think that God's judgement will never come. This is a grave miscalculation! The Bible tells us that God is slow to anger, not that he is *without* anger or unable to express anger. He is not indifferent to sin. Paul vehemently warned the Romans not to indulge in God's kindness or to mistake it as a lack of God's commitment to judge unrighteousness:

> So when you, a mere man, pass judgment on them and yet do the same things, do you think you will escape God's judgment? Or do you show contempt for the riches of his kindness, tolerance and patience, not realizing that God's kindness leads you toward repentance? But because of your stubbornness and your unrepentant heart, you are storing up wrath against yourself for the day of God's wrath, when his righteous judgment will be revealed (Rom. 2:3-5).

Are you behaving like the Ninevites? Do you think that God's judgement will not come? Are you storing up wrath for the day of wrath? If you are playing this game with God, end it now! Do not show contempt for God's graciousness. Nahum reminds us that there are limits to God's grace. Yes, God is a gracious God, but his grace is not infinite. As R.C. Sproul noted:

God's grace is not infinite. God is infinite and God is gracious. We experience the grace of an infinite God, but grace is not infinite. God sets limits to His patience and forbearance. He warns us over and over again that someday the ax will fall and his judgment will be poured out.[4]

Nahum reminds us that someday the axe will fall and on that day Jesus will come as a judge!

JESUS IS A WARRIOR

Nahum also speaks of God as a warrior who comes to conquer his enemies. Nahum describes God as a cloud rider who comes like a storm and utterly vanquishes his enemies. The prophet declares that when God comes in judgement the mountains will melt, the earth will tremble and no one will be able to stand on that day. Does this aspect of Nahum's prophecy have any connection to the work of Jesus Christ? Is Jesus depicted as a warrior in the New Testament? My answer is a resounding 'yes!' Let's look at a few examples from the New Testament which parallel the warrior themes of Nahum.

First, Nahum describes God as coming to make war by riding on the clouds (Nahum 1:3). The New Testament depicts Jesus as the great cloud rider. Note the language Jesus employs when he describes his second coming: 'At that time the sign of the Son of Man will appear in the sky, and all the nations of the earth will mourn. *They will see the Son of Man coming on the clouds of the sky*, with power and great glory' (Matt. 24:30, emphasis mine). When Jesus returns in judgement on the Last Great Day, he will come riding on the clouds.[5]

Secondly, Nahum depicts God's war-making power as impacting the entire earth. He tells us that God will make mountains melt, leave lands desolate and make the entire earth tremble (Nahum 1:4-5). Peter uses similar language to describe the return of Jesus Christ: 'But the day of the Lord will come like a thief. The heavens will disappear with a roar; the elements will be destroyed by fire, and the earth and everything in it will be laid bare' (2 Peter

3:10). Finally, Nahum states that when God comes to conquer his enemies none of them will survive; none will be able to withstand his indignation (Nahum 1:6). As you will recall, Nahum expresses this point by positing two rhetorical questions: 'Who can withstand his indignation? Who can endure his fierce anger?' (Nahum 1:6). In the book of Revelation, the apostle John poses a similar rhetorical question to describe the utter victory of the Lord Jesus Christ over his enemies: 'They called to the mountains and the rocks, "Fall on us and hide us from the face of him who sits on the throne and from the wrath of the Lamb! *For the great day of their wrath has come, and who can stand?*"' (Rev. 6:16-17, emphasis mine).

The New Testament reveals that Jesus is the great cloud rider and the great warrior who will shake the earth. It tells us that Jesus will return to make war: 'I saw heaven standing open and there before me was a white horse, whose rider is called Faithful and True. With justice he judges and *makes war*' (Rev. 19:11, emphasis mine). Although Jesus' work as a warrior will be most vividly manifested at his second coming, it would be a mistake to ignore his work as a warrior in this present age. The apostle Paul reminds us in 1 Corinthians 15:25 that Jesus is presently waging war against his enemies: 'For he must reign until he has put all his enemies under his feet.' Similarly, the Westminster Shorter Catechism notes that Jesus is currently 'ruling and defending us' and is presently 'restraining and conquering all his and our enemies'.[6] Finally, we also see Jesus' war-making power displayed in the victorious expansion of his kingdom throughout the world. In fact, every time a sinner comes to faith we are witnessing the war-making prowess of Jesus Christ. Jesus is our divine warrior!

In light of the fact that Jesus is such a powerful divine warrior, no one should desire to be his enemy. We too often wrongly think that those who are not serving Christ are in some neutral category. The Bible has only two categories: those who are subjects of Christ and those who are enemies of Christ. The scary thing is that we are all born as his enemies: 'Like the rest, we were by nature objects of wrath' (Eph. 2:3). The only way we can cease being an enemy of Christ is by becoming reconciled to him through his death, by believing in him. Paul makes this point in Romans 5:10: '...when we were God's enemies, we were reconciled to him through the death of his Son'. Those who believe in and serve Jesus are no longer his enemies. However, Paul tells us that those who do not serve Christ are destined for destruction: 'For, as I have often told you before and now say again even with tears, *many live as enemies of the cross of Christ. Their destiny is destruction*, their god is their stomach, and their glory is in their shame. Their mind is on earthly things' (Phil. 3:18-19, emphasis mine). In which category do you belong? Are you serving Jesus? Note the stern warning provided by the author of Hebrews to those who know the truth about Jesus, but choose to reject it: 'If we deliberately keep on sinning after we have received the knowledge of the truth, no sacrifice for sins is left, but only a fearful expectation of judgment and of raging fire that will consume the enemies of God' (Heb. 10:26-27). The Bible tells us that Jesus is coming to make war on his enemies. Make certain that you are his servant, rather than his enemy!

JESUS IS A DELIVERER

Nahum tells Judah to rejoice because God's judgement on their enemy Nineveh will result in their deliverance. God's victory over Nineveh liberated Judah. Nahum proclaims this liberation in his prophecy: 'Look, there on the mountains, the feet of one who brings good news, who proclaims peace! Celebrate your festivals, O Judah, and fulfill your vows. No more will the wicked invade you; they will be completely destroyed' (Nahum 1:15). Do you see what Nahum is saying here? He is telling the people that the destruction of the Ninevites will allow them to experience peace, celebrate their festivals and fulfil their vows. They will be able to worship God without fear of invasion from the wicked Ninevites. Are there any parallels to this liberation in the work of Jesus Christ?

In order to answer this question, we must first consider the nature of our enemies. In the New Testament we are told that our enemies are not particular nations or people, but rather are spiritual in nature: 'For our struggle is not against flesh and blood, but against the rulers, against the authorities, against the powers of this dark world and against the spiritual forces of evil in the heavenly realms' (Eph. 6:12). So who are our enemies? They are sin, Satan and death and the New Testament proclaims that Jesus came to deliver us from each of these enemies.

First, Jesus came to deliver us from sin. He is the Lamb of God who came to take away the sin of the world (John 1:29). Through Jesus we are no longer slaves to sin (Rom. 6:6). Paul tells us that through our union with Christ we 'have been set free from sin and have become slaves to righteousness' (Rom. 6:18). However, our victory over sin is not complete in this age. Although sin is no longer our master, we continue to struggle with it. The good news is that when Jesus returns we will be glorified and shall sin no more. Jesus delivers us from sin.

Secondly, Jesus came to deliver us from Satan. In the Gospel of Mark, Jesus drives out a demon from a man and the teachers of the law claim that Jesus did this by the power of Satan, stating, 'By the prince of demons he is driving out demons' (Mark 3:22). Listen to the response of Jesus to this accusation:

> So Jesus called them and spoke to them in parables: "How can Satan drive out Satan? If a kingdom is divided against itself, that kingdom cannot stand. If a house is divided against itself, that house cannot stand. And if Satan opposes himself and is divided, he cannot stand; his end has come. In fact, no one can enter a strong man's house and carry off his possessions unless he first ties up the strong man. Then he can rob his house (Mark 3:23-27).

By this parable, Jesus declared that he had bound the 'strong man' who is Satan. Jesus has limited Satan's power to interfere with the gospel and to destroy the spiritual life of the believer. However, Satan remains a threat to us in this age. Peter tells us that the devil is our enemy and seeks to devour us like a roaring lion (1 Peter 5:8). The good news is that Jesus promises that when he returns he will defeat Satan entirely and liberate us from his attacks (Rev. 20:10). Jesus delivers us from Satan.

Third, Jesus came to deliver us from death. We know that one of the penalties of Adam's first transgression is physical death. Paul reminds us that the 'wages of sin is death' (Rom. 6:23). Jesus came to deliver us from death by granting us eternal life: 'For God so loved the world that he gave his one and only Son, that whoever believes in him shall not perish but have eternal life' (John 3:16). Adam brought death, but the Last Adam, Jesus, brought life: 'For since death came through a man, the resurrection of the dead comes also through a man' (1 Cor. 15:21). However, much like Christ's victory over sin and Satan, his victory over death is only partially realized in this age. We still die physically, but the good news is that the sting of death is already removed (1 Cor. 15:55) and eventually death itself will be destroyed at Christ's return: 'For he must reign until he has put all his enemies under his feet. The last enemy to be destroyed is death' (1 Cor. 15:25-26). Jesus delivers his people from death.

In the book of Nahum the good news is that God's enemies are destined for destruction and God's people are destined for deliverance (1:7-8). It is important to remember that when Nahum spoke this promise the people had to wait to experience its fulfilment. Yet, the promise of this deliverance provided them with great comfort in their present circumstances. Similarly, Jesus' defeat of our enemies should fill us with great comfort in this present age. Even though we still struggle in this life against our enemies, we know the ultimate destiny of our enemies and we know our own ultimate destiny. Our enemies will be destroyed and we will be delivered. This knowledge should help us to live godly lives even in the face of fierce opposition from our enemies. Paul uses this exact argument in his letter to the suffering Christians in Philippi:

> 'Whatever happens, conduct yourselves in a manner worthy of the gospel of Christ. Then, whether I come and see you or only hear about you in my absence, I will know that you stand firm in one spirit, contending as one man for the faith of the gospel without being frightened in any

way by those who oppose you. This is a sign to them that they will be destroyed, but that you will be saved – and that by God' (Phil. 1:27-28).

Paul told the Philippian believers that they could withstand the persecutions of their enemies and live for Christ because their enemies will ultimately be destroyed and they will ultimately be delivered. The same is true for believers in our own age and that is good news indeed!

When God destroyed Nineveh, the people of Judah were set free to worship the living God. They could live for him without fear of invasion from their enemies. This message was received by the people of Israel as 'good news' (Nahum 1:15). So it is with the victorious work of Jesus on behalf of the church. Jesus has come to liberate his people from their enemies so that they might live for him. Jesus has delivered us from sin, Satan and death. This is good news for us and we should declare it to all (Rom. 10:14-16).

Is Night Falling for You?

Nahum is not a mere Old Testament story which should be shelved and forgotten, for the New Testament reveals that Jesus is a judge, warrior and deliverer. The message of Nahum is just as relevant today as it was in the seventh century B.C. because it reminds us that the time of God's grace is finite. It reminds us that the time to repent is now! It reminds us that the time to embrace Jesus is now! Just think about it for a moment. If invading the northern kingdom of Israel and deporting the people of God is an injustice which God meets with the swift and powerful judgement described in Nahum, what do you think he has in store for those who reject his only begotten Son?

How much more severely do you think a man deserves to be punished who has trampled the Son of God under foot, who has treated as an unholy thing the blood of the covenant that sanctified him, and who has insulted the

Spirit of grace? For we know him who said, 'It is mine to avenge; I will repay', and again, 'The Lord will judge his people.' It is a dreadful thing to fall into the hands of the living God (Heb. 10:29-31).

You are living in the time of Jonah, but the time of Nahum is coming!

Jonathan Edwards concluded his sermon 'Sinners in the Hands of an Angry God' with these words:

Therefore, let everyone that is out of Christ, now awake and fly from the wrath to come. The wrath of Almighty God is now undoubtedly hanging over a great part of this congregation. Let every one fly out of Sodom. Haste and escape for your lives, look not behind you, escape to the mountains, lest you be consumed.[7]

Night will fall on the day of grace and there is only one way to be spared from the wrath to come – believe in the Lord Jesus Christ. Make sure that you fly out of Sodom and enter the embrace of our Lord and Saviour! Then you too will know the comfort and good news declared by Nahum. That is how Nahum speaks of Jesus!

QUESTIONS FOR DISCUSSION

1. How does the prophecy of Nahum serve to correct unbalanced and erroneous views of God in our culture and in the church?

2. After Nahum describes the judgement which will befall Nineveh he declares that this is 'good news' for the people of God (Nahum 1:15). The words 'good news' are used in the Bible to describe the gospel of Jesus Christ (See Isaiah 52:7 and Romans 10:4-6). Nahum reminds us that God's judgement is part of the gospel message. Given this fact, what role should God's judgement play in our evangelism, both personal evangelism and evangelism from the pulpit?

3. Discuss how the following passages reveal Jesus' work as a divine warrior: Mark 1:12-13; Mark 1:23-28; Mark 5:1-20; Matthew 21:7-17; Colossians 2:14-15 and Acts 1:1-11.

4. The New Testament teaches that all believers, due to their rebirth and union with Christ, are drawn into a spiritual battle. Discuss how the following passages reveal the duty and role of believers in this spiritual battle: Romans 6:12-13; 2 Corinthians 10:3-5; Ephesians 6:10-17 and 2 Timothy 2:3-4.

5. One of the premises of this chapter is that judgement against God's enemies leads to deliverance for God's people. Can you think of any other Biblical examples of this dynamic?

Chapter 8

LIVING BY FAITH: HABAKKUK

As I AM WRITING THIS BOOK, my wife and I are in the process of adopting a child from China. International adoption is a complicated, expensive and arduous process. It begins with a flurry of paperwork and a rush to get that paperwork filed with the proper authorities. However, once that initial paperwork is complete and your dossier is sent to the foreign nation, you then begin a period of waiting. Then you wait, wait and wait some more. My wife and I are currently living in this period of waiting. We have the promise of a child, but we must wait to realize that promise. We are currently living in the gap between promise and fulfilment. The prophecy of Habakkuk addresses a similar theme. Habakkuk speaks of the challenge of living between promise and fulfilment in the kingdom of God. He reminds us that in order to traverse the gap between promise and fulfilment we must live by faith, not by an abstract or empty faith, but a faith filled with biblical content and focused upon Jesus Christ.

ENTERING INTO HABAKKUK'S WORLD

We know very little about Habakkuk. He may have been a Levite, possibly a temple singer.[1] We are certain that he prophesied in the latter part of the seventh century B.C. and that he lived during a time of upheaval. He experienced the glorious revival which occurred during the reign of King Josiah (640-609 B.C.), but he also experienced the spiritual decline that ensued in Judah after Josiah's death. He witnessed the fall of the city of Nineveh (612 B.C.) and the decline of the Assyrian empire, but he also observed the rise of the Babylonian empire.

As the sixth century B.C. dawned, Judah faced two great enemies which threatened to destroy them. The first enemy was internal. Judah had reached new spiritual lows under the reign of King Jehoiakim and their own sinfulness endangered their relationship with God. The second enemy was external. The Babylonians were a constant threat to the safety and integrity of Judah. It was into this setting that God sent Habakkuk to prophesy to his people.

THE PROPHET'S MESSAGE: A JOURNEY FROM PROMISE TO FULFILMENT

Habakkuk's prophecy is similar to the prophecies of Jonah and Hosea, because like these other prophets, Habakkuk is not just called to deliver a message, but also to live it. Habakkuk bears the burden of a journey of faith. He must personally live in the gap between promise and fulfilment. The prophecy of Habakkuk tells the tale of the prophet's personal struggle as he moves from the depths of despair to hope in a present promise and to faith in a future fulfilment.

The prophecy of Habakkuk commences with deep despair. In fact, it begins with the prophet crying out to God: 'How long, O LORD, must I call for help, but you do not listen? Or cry out to you, "Violence!" but you do not save?' (Hab. 1:2).[2] In verse

3, the prophet describes the source of his lament as the fact that God has not addressed the extreme wickedness of Judah: 'Why do you make me look at injustice? Why do you tolerate wrong? Destruction and violence are before me; there is strife, and conflict abounds.' Habakkuk is vexed over the injustice which is occurring in Judah and he does not understand why God is not acting to remedy the situation. He continues and expands his lament in verse 4: 'Therefore the law is paralyzed, and justice never prevails. The wicked hem in the righteous, so that justice is perverted.' According to the perspective of Habakkuk, the world is crumbling around him and God seems to be an uninterested spectator.

God, however, is not uninterested and he soon comes to answer the questions of his distressed prophet. He explains to Habakkuk that he will address his concerns regarding the wickedness of Judah. God describes how he will do so in Habakkuk 1:5-6:

> Look at the nations and watch – and be utterly amazed. For I am going to do something in your days that you would not believe, even if you were told. I am raising up the Babylonians, that ruthless and impetuous people, who sweep across the whole earth to seize dwelling places not their own.

Do you understand the substance of God's reply to Habakkuk? God informed Habakkuk that his means of redressing Judah's wickedness would be to send the Babylonians against them. God told Habakkuk that he would correct the unrighteousness of his people by allowing the Babylonians to conquer them and to take them into captivity. This was clearly not the answer the prophet expected or desired! Habakkuk was utterly bewildered by God's radical plan to use the 'ruthless and impetuous' Babylonians to remedy Judah's ills. His bewilderment is evidenced by his interrogation of God in chapter 1, verse 13: 'Your eyes are too pure to look on evil; you cannot tolerate wrong. Why then do you tolerate the treacherous? Why are you silent while the wicked swallow up those more righteous than themselves?' By means of these questions Habakkuk lodged his complaint with God. He then climbed a watchtower to await the answer of the Lord: 'I will stand at my watch and station myself on the ramparts; I will look to see what he will say to me, and what answer I am to give to this complaint' (Hab. 2:1).

Again, God provided the prophet with a direct answer. He gave Habakkuk a promise that the Babylonian captivity would be temporary and that after a set period of time God would deliver his people. God explained this to Habakkuk in these words: 'For the revelation awaits an appointed time; it speaks of the end and will not prove false. Though it linger, wait for it; it will certainly come and will not delay' (Hab. 2:3). God's promise was that he would deliver his people in the future. But do you see a problem? God's deliverance is a present promise, but its fulfilment remains in the future. The promise is certain, but the Babylonians are still coming! Habakkuk and the people of Judah are called to wait; they are called to live in the gap between promise and fulfilment. The question that arises is, 'How are they going to make it? How are they going to survive in the gap between promise and fulfilment?'

God provides the answer to this question in Habakkuk 2:4: 'See, he is puffed up; his desires are not upright – *but the righteous will live by his faith*' (emphasis mine). God informed Habakkuk and the people of Judah that there is only one way to survive in the gap between promise and fulfilment – by faith. The only way they could make it through the dark days of the Babylonian captivity was to live by faith in the promises of God, believing that God would do what he said he would do. This is the existential struggle of Habakkuk and the people of Judah. It is this struggle which connects the modern believer to the prophecy of Habakkuk and it is this struggle which turns our eyes to Jesus.

IN JESUS WE PERSEVERE BY FAITH

I hope you can already see how relevant this message is for us to-day. New Testament believers are in a very similar situation to that of Habakkuk and the believers of his time. We too live in the gap between promise and fulfilment. Like Habakkuk, we see the injustice, violence and wickedness all around us. We see the wicked prosper and the righteous hemmed in on all sides. Haven't you ever cried out, 'How long, O Lord?' Haven't you ever climbed the watchtower waiting for an answer from God? Habakkuk is talking about real life; he is talking about having faith in God in the face of despair. This is a timeless message. It is as relevant today as it was when God spoke it through his prophet Habakkuk. Willem VanGemeren notes the timelessness of Habakkuk's message: 'The book of Habakkuk challenges the righteous to discern God's will in adverse times and calls for perseverance while awaiting the establishment of God's righteous kingdom.'[3] You are in the very same position in this present age. You too live between promise and fulfilment because you live between the two advents of Christ. The people of Judah were waiting for deliverance from Babylon and you are waiting for the deliverance that will accompany the return of Christ.

The New Testament teaches us that the only way we can make the journey from promise to fulfilment is by faith. That's why the writer to the Hebrews quotes from Habakkuk to encourage and admonish us to persevere in faith as we await the fulfilment of God's promises at the return of Christ:

> So do not throw away your confidence; it will be richly rewarded. You need to persevere so that when you have done the will of God, you will receive what he has promised. For in just a very little while, 'He who is coming will come and will not delay. But my righteous one will live by faith. And if he shrinks back, I will not be pleased with him' (Heb. 10:35-38).

It is important for us to understand that this type of persevering faith is only meaningful in the gap between promise and fulfilment. This type of faith will have no meaning in the time of fulfilment when we possess the full reality of the promise. Remember what the book of Hebrews tells us: 'Now faith is being sure of *what we hope for* and certain of *what we do not see*' (Heb. 11:1, emphasis mine). Essentially, the writer to the Hebrews is telling us that faith is about living as if the future fulfilment is a present reality. A.S. Peake describes the dynamics of Biblical faith as follows:

> Faith has this quality – that it can lift us into fellowship with the Unseen, that it can carry us within the veil … Faith thus has a power of realization, by which the invisible becomes visible and the future becomes present. While hope is the confident anticipation of a future regarded as future, faith appropriates that future as an experience of the present.[4]

Scripture states over and over again that faith is proved in the trials and travails of this present age. Note the words of James: 'Consider it pure joy, my brothers, whenever you face trials of many kinds, because you know that the testing of your faith develops perseverance' (James 1:2). Peter makes a similar point: 'These have come so that your faith – of greater worth than gold, which perishes even though refined by fire – may be proved genuine and may result in praise, glory and honor when Jesus Christ is revealed' (1 Peter 1:7). Paul succinctly summarizes this principle as follows: 'We live by faith, not by sight' (2 Cor. 5:7). Do you see the point? Our faith is proved in those most desperate moments of life. It is proved in the gap between promise and fulfilment. It is proved when we lose our job, when our spouse deserts us, when we hear the diagnosis and when we stand over the coffin.

Perhaps you're thinking, 'I just can't do it. I don't have faith like that. When trials hit I wither.' Well, you are not alone. Even the disciples who had Jesus in their immediate presence struggled with persevering faith. Do you remember how they panicked on the boat in the midst of the storm? Do you remember the words of Jesus to them? 'He replied, "You of little faith, why are you so afraid?"' (Matt. 8:26). We all struggle in our journey of faith. None of us can make this voyage from promise to fulfilment in our own power. The good news is that Jesus carries us through the gap from promise to fulfilment.

The Bible teaches us that our ultimate destiny is not based on our faithfulness, but rather on his. The New Testament reminds us of this fact in numerous places. Note where Paul puts his confidence when he is in the midst of suffering: 'That is why I am suffering as I am. Yet I am not ashamed, because I know whom I have believed, and *am convinced that he is able to guard what I have entrusted to him for that day*' (2 Tim. 1:12, emphasis mine). Paul could endure the suffering of this present age because he believed that Jesus would carry him to the day of fulfilment. Paul expresses a similar confidence in his benediction in 1 Thessalonians: 'May God himself, the God of peace, sanctify you through and through. May your whole spirit, soul and body be kept blameless at the coming of our Lord Jesus Christ. *The one who calls you is faithful and he will do it*' (1 Thess. 5:23-24, emphasis mine). Paul did not admonish the Thessalonians to persevere by their own faith, but rather he encouraged them to place their trust in the faithfulness of Jesus Christ. Finally, Jude reminds us in his benediction that Jesus is the only one who can carry us from promise to fulfilment: '*To him who is able to keep you from falling and to present you before his glorious presence without fault and with great joy* – to the only God our Savior be glory, majesty, power and authority, through Jesus Christ our Lord, before all ages, now and forevermore! Amen' (Jude 1:24, emphasis mine). We will persevere in faith because of the faithfulness of Jesus. He will guard us on our journey. He is faithful and he will do it. He is able to keep us from falling. He will present us before his glorious presence. We will make it through the gap between promise and fulfilment because Jesus will carry us across the divide!

So how do we stay strong in our faith while we are in the midst of trials? How can we keep ourselves focused on Jesus and his promises, rather than on the fact that the Babylonians are coming? The answer to that question is the same for us as it was for the people of God in Habakkuk's day. An interesting thing occurred when God gave his promise of deliverance to Habakkuk. God commanded Habakkuk to preserve his promises in writing: 'Then the LORD replied: "Write down the revelation and make it plain on tablets so that a herald may run with it"' (Hab. 2:2). Why did God command that his promise be written down? First, it was an indication that this promise was not solely for the prophet. God instructed that the promise be written so that it could be heralded to the whole nation. Second, he commanded that it be committed to writing because he wanted the people to remember his promise even during the bleak trials of the Babylonian captivity. He wanted them to be able to grasp onto his written promise. God commanded that his promises be written down so that they could be both proclaimed and preserved. Just like Judah, we too have the promises of God written for us in the Bible and God has sent heralds to constantly remind us about his promises as we traverse through the gap between promise and reality. In times of trial, make certain that you are close to God's Word. Do not neglect your personal devotions or hearing the word preached in your local congregation. It is vital for us to rehearse and remember the promises of God. We can survive in the gap by embracing these promises through faith.

Finally, as you struggle in the gap between promise and fulfilment, look to Jesus for your strength. He will carry you. Heed the words of the author of Hebrews who encouraged his people with these words: 'Let us fix our eyes on Jesus, *the author and perfecter of our faith*, who for the joy set before him endured the cross, scorning its shame, and sat down at the right hand of the throne of God' (Heb. 12:2, emphasis mine). Jesus not only gives you faith, but he perfects your faith. In Jesus, you will persevere by faith!

IN JESUS WE LIVE BY FAITH

We have seen that in Jesus we persevere by faith; we can make it through the gap from promise to fulfilment. This is the existential aspect of our faith. Each day we live by this persevering faith. We endure the trials of life by clinging to the one who is able to keep us from falling. However, the prophecy of Habakkuk points to another aspect of our faith, for when Habakkuk states that 'the righteous will live by his faith' he is not only speaking of surviving the trials of this age, but of a deeper and more powerful aspect of faith. He is telling us that we live by faith, not only existentially, but also eternally. In other words, faith not only carries us through the gap from promise to fulfilment, but it also carries us from death to life. Habakkuk tells us that the spiritually dead can live by faith.

We know the Bible teaches us that we are dead. God told Adam that if he ate of the tree of the knowledge of good and evil he would surely die (Gen. 2:17). Paul tells us in Romans that through Adam's transgression, death and sin came to all men (Rom. 5:12). Paul tells us in Ephesians that we begin this life dead: 'As for you, *you were dead* in your transgressions and sins' (Eph. 2:1, emphasis mine). We are all born under a death sentence: 'For the wages of sin is death' (Rom. 6:23). Habakkuk's prophecy speaks hope to those who are on spiritual death row. He proclaims the promise that the righteous will live by faith. That is, they will live before God eternally by faith in Jesus Christ.

It is interesting to note that the New Testament quotes Habakkuk's words 'the righteous will live by his faith' three times. In the previous section of this chapter, we examined one of these references from the book of Hebrews. As we saw, in Hebrews 10:38 the author uses Habakkuk's words to illustrate the persevering (or existential) aspect of living by faith. Note the italicized words which immediately follow the quotation from Habakkuk: 'But my righteous one will live by faith. *And if he shrinks back, I will not be pleased with him*' (Heb. 10:38, emphasis mine). The writer to the Hebrews is clearly admonishing New Testament believers to persevere by faith and to not shrink back. He is telling them to forge ahead to the day of fulfilment.

The other two references to Habakkuk's words in the New Testament deal with the second aspect of living by faith which we are pondering in this section. Paul refers to Habakkuk's words in two of his letters, Romans and Galatians, and his point is exactly the same in each epistle. In Romans, Paul uses the words of Habakkuk to define how believers receive the glorious benefits of the gospel of Jesus Christ: 'For in the gospel a righteousness from God is revealed, a righteousness that is by faith from first to last, just as it is written: "The righteous will live by faith"' (Rom. 1:17). Essentially, Paul tells us that we are saved through faith.

Likewise in Galatians, Paul again quotes Habakkuk's words to illustrate that justification is attained through faith in Jesus Christ rather than through the believer's keeping of the law: 'Clearly no one is justified before God by the law, because, "The righteous will live by faith"' (Gal. 3:11). Do you see what Paul is saying in these passages? He is telling us that by faith in Jesus Christ we can live spiritually and eternally! Under the inspiration of the Holy Spirit, Paul understood the words of Habakkuk as not only speaking of persevering faith, but also of saving faith. It is this faith, which is a gift of God (Eph. 2:8), that serves as the instrument which brings to us the blessings of Christ's work. The *Westminster Confession of Faith* describes the nature of saving faith as follows: 'But the principal acts of saving faith are accepting, receiving, and resting upon Christ alone for justification, sanctification, and eternal life, by virtue of the covenant of grace.'[5]

Perhaps you are thinking to yourself that Paul extends Habakkuk's words far beyond their original meaning and context by applying them to the gospel of Jesus Christ. After all, wasn't Habakkuk's main concern the deliverance of Judah from the oncoming Babylonian captivity? Here we encounter an aspect of typology known as escalation.[6] The original type, deliverance from Babylon, is far exceeded by its antitype, deliverance from the wrath of God. Listen to how the Scottish theologian Robert Haldane (1764-1842) described this dynamic in his classic commentary on the book of Romans. He noted the following regarding Paul's use of Habakkuk in Romans 1:17:

> The passage itself is quoted from the prophecies of Habakkuk, and is generally supposed to relate, in its primary sense, to the deliverance from the Babylonian captivity, which was a type of the deliverance obtained by the Gospel. Through faith in the Divine promises the first was obtained, and the second in like manner is obtained through faith. But in whatever sense the Prophet used these words, the Apostle, speaking by the same Spirit, assigns them to their just and legitimate extension. They are true in respect to an earthly and temporal deliverance,

and they are equally true in respect to a spiritual deliverance.[7]

By its use in the New Testament, the prophecy of Habakkuk reveals the glorious doctrine of justification by faith alone. It is no wonder that these words of Habakkuk played such a powerful role in the Protestant Reformation. Many consider that the Reformation began when Luther's eyes were opened by Habakkuk's words reiterated by Paul in Romans 1:17. In 1515, after studying Romans 1:17, Luther wrote:

Night and day I pondered till I saw the connection between the justice of God and the statement that 'the just shall live by his faith'. Then I grasped that the justice of God is that righteousness by which through grace and sheer mercy God justifies us through faith. Thereupon I felt myself to be reborn and to have gone through open doors into paradise.[8]

Two years later Luther nailed his Ninety-five Theses on the door at Wittenberg and Europe was turned upside down. It is amazing to consider that these seven words from this minor prophet, 'the just shall live by his faith', have had such a profound impact, not only on theology, but on the entire course of Western Civilization.

While we indeed live by faith, it is important to recognize that this faith has no power in itself. Saving faith brings life to us only because it is the instrument, or channel, which God uses to impute the righteousness of Jesus Christ to us. Listen to how Pastor Edward Donnelly describes the connection between faith and Christ's righteousness:

Faith as an instrument is the link between sinner and Saviour, the channel through which the benefits of his life and death are imputed to us. It could be compared to a surgeon's scalpel, the means through which his expertise invades and heals our bodies. In itself, it is worthless. In the wrong hands, it could kill. But, when taken by the surgeon, it is a life-saver. Yet it is he who saves us, not the instrument he uses.[9]

We live by faith solely because it is the means by which we receive Christ and his righteousness.

The New Testament teaches us, through the words of Habakkuk, that the only way to live eternally with God is to embrace the Lord Jesus Christ and his righteousness through the gift of faith. As Jesus declared in the Gospel of John, 'For my Father's will is that everyone who looks to the Son and believes in him shall have eternal life, and I will raise him up at the last day' (John 6:40). In Jesus, we live by faith!

In Jesus We Know by Faith

So far in this chapter we have seen that we persevere by faith and live eternally by faith. However, there is a third aspect of faith which is revealed in the prophecy of Habakkuk. In the first thirteen verses of the second chapter of his prophecy, Habakkuk pronounces a series of woes against the wicked nation of Babylon. Babylon had persecuted the kingdom of God and Habakkuk was declaring to them that they would ultimately be judged for this persecution. However, in the middle of these woes Habakkuk makes the following declaration: 'For the earth will be filled with the knowledge of the glory of the LORD, as the waters cover the sea' (Hab. 2:14). The promise of this verse is that one day the knowledge of the Lord will ultimately fill the whole earth, but the question is when and how will this occur?

The New Testament provides the answers to these questions. First, it reveals that the promise of Habakkuk 2:14 is fulfilled in the age of the Messiah.[10] Second, it also tells us how this promise will be fulfilled. The New Testament declares that the knowledge of the Lord becomes a global reality through the combination of the gift of faith and the preaching of the Word of God. These two things, faith and the preaching of the Word, go hand in hand in the extension of the knowledge of the Lord to the whole earth.

Faith in Christ requires knowledge of Christ. Biblical faith is not an empty faith, but rather it is filled with content. John Murray (1898-1975) noted this interrelationship between faith and knowledge: 'We must know who Christ is, what he has done, and what he is able to do. Otherwise faith would be blind conjecture at the best and foolish mockery at the worst. There must be apprehension of the truth respecting Christ.'[11] The New Testament explains that we apprehend the truth about Jesus through the combination of faith and the preaching of God's Word. Note how the Apostle Paul brings faith and the preaching of the Word together in the tenth chapter of the epistle to the Romans:

> As the Scripture says, 'Anyone who trusts in him will never be put to shame.' For there is no difference between Jew and Gentile – the same Lord is Lord of all and richly blesses all who call on him, for, 'Everyone who calls on the name of the Lord will be saved.' How, then, can they call on the one they have not believed in? And how can they believe in the one of whom they have not heard? And how can they hear without someone preaching to them? And how can they preach unless they are sent? As it is written, 'How beautiful are the feet of those who bring good news!' But not all the Israelites accepted the good news. For Isaiah says, 'Lord, who has believed our message?' *Consequently, faith comes from hearing the message, and the message is heard through the word of Christ.* (Rom. 10:11-17, emphasis mine)

In this passage Paul is revealing the intimate nexus which exists between faith and the Word of God. The knowledge of the Lord is spread throughout the earth by preaching and it is appropriated by faith. The Westminster Confession of Faith makes a similar point when it states that it is only by faith that 'a Christian believeth to be true whatsoever is revealed in the Word'.[12] Therefore, the combination of faith and the preaching of the Word is vital to the extension of the knowledge of the Lord to all the earth.

These two forces, faith and the preaching of God's Word, are essential components of the kingdom work of the risen Christ. This reality is displayed in the Great Commission in which Jesus authorizes and commands the spread of the knowledge of the Lord throughout the entire earth:

> Then Jesus came to them and said, 'All authority in heaven and on earth has been given to me. Therefore go and make disciples of all nations, baptizing them in the name of the Father and of the Son and of the Holy Spirit, and teaching them to obey everything I have commanded you. And surely I am with you always, to the very end of the age' (Matt. 28:18-20).

This Great Commission begins to be fulfilled in the book of Acts which commences with the victorious Messiah ascending to heaven. Before he ascends, however, Jesus made the following declaration to his disciples: 'But you will receive power when the Holy Spirit comes on you; and you will be my witnesses in Jerusalem, and in all Judea and Samaria, *and to the ends of the earth*' (Acts 1:8, emphasis mine). The remainder of the book of Acts explains how this verse was fulfilled; it tells us how the knowledge of the Lord spread to the ends of the earth.

First, the knowledge of the Lord came to Jerusalem and Judea on the Day of Pentecost (Acts 2). On the Day of Pentecost Peter preached the Word of God and called on the Jews to believe in Jesus Christ (Acts 2:38-41). Next, the knowledge of the Lord came to Samaria through Philip's preaching of Christ (Acts 8:5). After this event, the knowledge of the Lord extended to the ends of the earth through the conversions of the Ethiopian Eunuch (Acts 8:26-40) and the Roman Centurion Cornelius (Acts 10), both of whom were Gentiles. Then the knowledge of the Lord continued to spread in a powerful way through the three missionary journeys of Paul (Acts 13-21:14). The book of Acts concludes with Paul in prison in Rome, but even his imprisonment is unable to restrain the spread of the knowledge of the Lord. The final verse in Acts records that even while imprisoned Paul 'preached the kingdom of God and taught about the Lord Jesus Christ' (Acts 28:31). The book of Acts reveals how the preaching of the Word and the gift of faith are instrumental to the spreading of the knowledge of the Lord throughout the whole earth.

The New Testament informs us that Habakkuk 2:14 is fulfilled through the kingdom of Jesus Christ. Jesus is ultimately the one who disseminates the knowledge of the Lord through his ordained means of faith and the Word of God. It is through Jesus, and him alone, that we receive the knowledge of the Lord, 'For God, who said, "Let light shine out of darkness", made his light shine in our hearts to give us *the light of the knowledge of the glory of God in the face of Christ*' (2 Cor. 4:6, emphasis mine). Through faith in Jesus Christ and his message, the believer and the world are filled with the knowledge of the glory of God! In Jesus, we know by faith.

Embrace the Promises

In this chapter we learned about the power of faith. First, we learned that we persevere by faith through Jesus. We can make it through the gap from promise to fulfilment because he is faithful to us. Second, we learned that we live, spiritually and eternally, through faith in Jesus Christ. Finally, we learned that faith is the means by which the knowledge of the Lord is spread throughout the entire world. Faith is a powerful gift. It is a gift given to us by God himself. It is given to us so that we might be delivered. It is interesting to note that Habakkuk's name means to 'embrace'. This is really the message of Habakkuk. The message is to embrace Jesus Christ and his promises by faith, for through faith in him comes life abundant and eternal. This is how Habakkuk speaks of Jesus!

Questions for Discussion

1. Try to list some events in your own life which required you to live in the gap between promise and fulfilment. Discuss how your faith in God helped you to persevere through this time.

2. In this chapter we discussed the great Reformation doctrine of justification by faith alone. However, this doctrine is easily threatened, as Martin Luther himself noted:

> I have myself taught this doctrine for twenty years, both in my preaching and my writings; and yet the old and tenacious mire clings to me, so that I find myself wanting to come to God bringing something in my hand, for which He should bestow his grace upon me. I cannot attain to casting myself on pure and simple grace only, and yet this is highly necessary.[13]

In this quotation, Luther noted how he often desired to bring something in his hand to God. What types of things might we try to bring to God to supplement our faith? Why is this wrong?

3. The prophecy of Habakkuk contains the promise that the knowledge of the Lord shall fill the whole earth (Hab. 2:14). In this chapter we saw how this began through the work of Christ and his apostles. However, this prophecy continues to be fulfilled in our own day. Discuss how you and your church can participate in the continuing spread of the knowledge of the Lord to all the earth.

4. The phrase 'anointed one' (or 'messiah') occurs thirty-nine times in the Old Testament. While most of the occurrences of this phrase in the Old Testament relate to the general use of the phrase (referring to leaders such as prophets, priests and kings), there are nine occurrences where the word is used to refer directly and specifically to *the* 'anointed one', Jesus Christ. One of these nine occurrences is in Habakkuk's prophecy (3:13). The other eight occurrences are found in the following passages: 1 Samuel 2:10, 35; Psalms 2:2; 20:6; 28:8; 84:9; and Daniel 9:25, 26. Read all nine of these passages and note what each reference reveals about the work of Jesus Christ.

Chapter 9

A TALE OF TWO DAYS: ZEPHANIAH

Thomas of Celaeno was a thirteenth-century Franciscan monk. He was a follower of St Francis of Assisi and eventually became his biographer. Celaeno is also credited with composing the famous Latin hymn *Dies Irae* ('The Day of Wrath'). In this hymn, Celaeno describes the Day of Judgement in vivid detail. The prophecy of Zephaniah served as one of the major sources for the imagery of Celaeno's hymn. Zephaniah was a rich source for this hymn because, more than any other minor prophet, he emphasizes the significance of the Day of the Lord. However, there is more to Zephaniah's prophecy than judgement. Zephaniah also speaks of a second day, a new day of hope and restoration. Both the Day of Judgement and the new day find their ultimate meaning in the person and work of Jesus Christ.

ENTERING INTO ZEPHANIAH'S WORLD

Like many of the minor prophets, we know very little about Zephaniah. We do know that he prophesied in the latter part of the seventh century B.C. during the early years of the reign of King Josiah. As you will recall from the chapter on Habakkuk, King Josiah was destined to become a great reformer in Judah.[1] However, Zephaniah prophesied during the early years of Josiah's reign when Judah was still in a period of spiritual decline.

The low spiritual state of Judah is described in the first chapter of Zephaniah's prophecy. He first attacks the religious and civil leadership by charging the priests with idolatry (1:4) and the civil leaders with unfaithfulness (1:8-9). Next, Zephaniah summarizes the spiritual condition of the entire nation. In Zephaniah 1:12, we learn that the people had become 'complacent' and did not believe God would intervene to change the situation. Zephaniah described the mindset of the people as follows: 'The Lord will do nothing, either good or bad' (Zeph. 1:12). The nation's leaders were rife with corruption and the average citizen was complacent. It was into this setting that God sent Zephaniah.

Before we discuss the specific message, it would be helpful to briefly deal with an issue which often arises in scholarly discussions of Zephaniah. As you read the prophecy, it will become immediately apparent to you that there is something very familiar about his prophecy. First, the major theme is the judgement of God which is a common theme among the Minor Prophets. Second, he deals with this common theme by using language which is very similar to that of other prophets. In fact, there is so much that is familiar about Zephaniah's prophecy that certain liberal scholars have criticized Zephaniah for his lack of originality. However, I believe that the repetition present in Zephaniah's prophecy is not due to a lack of originality, but rather is attributable to the unique role which Zephaniah's prophecy plays in the corpus of the Minor Prophets. It is important to remember that Zephaniah is the last of the pre-exilic prophets. This means that his prophecy represents the last warning to Judah before the Babylonian invasion and subsequent captivity. I think it is Zephaniah's unique place in the sequence of the Minor Prophets which accounts for the repetition present in his prophecy. His function is to summarize the themes of those prophets who preceded him. He represents one last cumulative warning to the people of God that judgement is coming![2]

THE PROPHET'S MESSAGE: TWO CONTRASTING DAYS

In the first section of Zephaniah's prophecy he speaks in horrifying detail about a coming day of judgement which he refers to four times as the 'Day of the Lord' (1:7; 1:14; 2:2 & 2:3). Zephaniah describes two main characteristics which will mark this terrible day.

First, Zephaniah declares that the Day of the Lord will be universal in scope; it will apply to everything:

> 'I will sweep away everything from the face of the earth', declares the LORD. 'I will sweep away both men and animals; I will sweep away the birds of the air and the fish of the sea. The wicked will have only heaps of rubble when I cut off man from the face of the earth', declares the LORD (Zeph. 1:2).

This language is reminiscent of another of God's previous judgements. Think back to Genesis and the time of Noah: 'So the LORD said, "I will wipe mankind, whom I have created, from the face of the earth – men and animals, and creatures that move along the ground, and birds of the air – for I am grieved that I have made them"' (Gen. 6:7). Zephaniah tells us that the Day of the Lord will be like the great flood in the days of Noah; it will be universal in scope!

Secondly, Zephaniah declares that the Day of the Lord will be comprehensive in its severity: 'That day will be a *day* of wrath, a *day* of distress and anguish, a *day* of trouble and ruin, a *day* of darkness and gloom, a *day* of clouds and blackness, a *day* of trumpet and battle cry against the fortified cities and against the corner towers' (Zeph. 1:15-16, emphasis mine). Do you notice a subtle reference to the creation account of Genesis here? The word 'day' is used six times in these two verses to describe the nature of the Day of the Lord. Some commentators believe that Zephaniah is comparing the comprehensive destructive power of the Day of the Lord to the comprehensive creative power of creation.[3]

The comprehensive nature of the Day of the Lord is also revealed in Zephaniah 3:8: '"Therefore wait for me", declares the LORD, "for the day I will stand up to testify. I have decided to assemble the nations, to gather the kingdoms and to pour out my wrath on them – all my fierce anger. *The whole world will be consumed by the fire of my jealous anger.*"' (emphasis mine). Clearly, the Day of the Lord will be all encompassing in its severity.

Zephaniah's prophecy is dominated by the imagery of judgement, but it is not without hope. In the closing verses of his prophecy, Zephaniah describes another coming day, a day of hope and restoration. He declares that there will be a day when people from all nations will worship God: 'Then will I purify the lips of the peoples, that all of them may call on the name of the LORD and serve him shoulder to shoulder. From beyond the rivers of Cush my worshipers, my scattered people, will bring me offerings' (Zeph. 3:9-10).[4] Zephaniah also promises that in this new day God will make humility an attribute of his people: 'On that day you will not be put to shame for all the wrongs you have done to me, because I will remove from this city those who rejoice in their pride. Never again will you be haughty on my holy hill. But I will leave within you the meek and humble, who trust in the name of the LORD' (Zeph. 3:11-12). Furthermore, in this new day holiness will be an attribute of God's people: 'The remnant of Israel will do no wrong; they will speak no lies, nor will deceit be found in their mouths. They will eat and lie down and no one will make them afraid' (Zeph. 3:13).[5] In the new day described by Zephaniah, God's people will include all nations; they will be humble and they will be holy.

We have seen that the prophecy of Zephaniah tells a tale of two days, a day of judgement and a day of restoration. Indeed, shortly after Zephaniah delivered his prophecy Judah experienced the judgement of the Lord. The Babylonians conquered Judah and took the people into captivity. Later, fifty years after the Babylonian invasion, Judah experienced a day of hope and restoration as the people returned from their exile in Babylon. The question raised by the prophecy of Zephaniah is: 'Does the Babylonian exile and subsequent return from exile fulfil the two days spoken of in this prophecy?' Well my answer is a qualified 'yes'. The Babylonian captivity and subsequent return partially fulfilled the prophecy of Zephaniah, but these events did not capture its fulness. Think about it for a moment. Did the Babylonian invasion match the description of the Day of the Lord given by Zephaniah? Was it universal in scope? Was it comprehensive in its severity? Also, consider the return from exile. Did all nations come and worship the Lord? Did the people of God become marked by humility and holiness? I contend that the two days described by Zephaniah were only partially fulfilled by the Babylonian captivity and the subsequent return from exile. The ultimate fulfilment of these two days is to be found in the person and work of Jesus Christ.[6] This is how the prophecy of Zephaniah turns our eyes to Jesus. He is the Lord of the ultimate Day of Judgement and he is the Lord of the ultimate new day of restoration.

JESUS IS LORD OF THE COMING DAY OF JUDGEMENT

As we have seen, Zephaniah's prophecy begins with a detailed description of a coming day of judgement which he refers to as the Day of the Lord. Zephaniah describes this day as being universal in scope and comprehensive in its severity. The Babylonian captivity was certainly a cataclysmic event in the history of Israel, but it did not fully capture the universality and comprehensiveness of the Day of the Lord described by Zephaniah. However, the New Testament describes a final Day of Judgement which does live up to the words of this prophecy. The New Testament ties this final Day of Judgement to the return of Jesus Christ. The following are two examples of how the New Testament connects the concept of the Day of the Lord to Christ's return:

• He will keep you strong to the end, so that you will be blameless on the *day of our Lord Jesus Christ* (1 Cor. 1:8, emphasis mine).

• Being confident of this, that he who began a good work in you will carry it on to completion *until the day of Christ Jesus* (Phil. 1:6, emphasis mine).

• *Concerning the coming of our Lord Jesus Christ* and our being gathered to him, we ask you, brothers, not to become easily unsettled or alarmed by some prophecy, report or letter supposed to have come from us, saying that the *day of the Lord* has already come (2 Thessalonians 2:1-2, emphasis mine).[7]

The New Testament informs us that Jesus is the Lord of the ultimate Day of the Lord. The New Testament not only applies the phrase 'Day of the Lord' to the final judgement by Jesus, it also applies the characteristics of universality and comprehensiveness. The New Testament declares that the final Day of the Lord will be universal in scope. For example, on the day of our Lord Jesus Christ everyone will acknowledge his Lordship. Philippians 2:10 tells us that on that day 'every knee' will bow 'in heaven and on earth and under the earth'. In addition, on the day of our Lord Jesus Christ there will be a universal judgement. The New Testament states three times that Jesus will judge everyone, including the living and the dead (Acts 10:42, 2 Tim. 4:1, and 1 Peter 4:5). Finally, the New Testament, like the prophecy of Zephaniah, links the Day of the Lord to the universal judgement experienced in the time of Noah: 'As it was in the days of Noah, so it will be at the coming of the Son of Man' (Matt. 24:37). The day of our Lord Jesus Christ will be universal in scope.

The New Testament also depicts the final Day of the Lord as comprehensive in its severity. According to the New Testament, this day will be all encompassing and intense. Note the language of the apostle Peter as he describes the severity of this day: 'But the day of the Lord will come like a thief. The heavens will disappear with a roar; the elements will be destroyed by fire, and the earth and everything in it will be laid bare' (2 Peter 3:10). The apostle John uses even more vivid and provocative imagery to describe the severity of this day:

> I watched as he opened the sixth seal. There was a great earthquake. The sun turned black like sackcloth made of goat hair, the whole moon turned blood red, and the stars in the sky fell to earth, as late figs drop from a fig tree when shaken by a strong wind. The sky receded like a scroll, rolling up, and every mountain and island was removed from its place. Then the kings of the earth, the princes, the generals, the rich, the mighty, and every slave and every free man hid in caves and among the rocks of the mountains. They called to the mountains and the rocks, 'Fall on us and hide us from the face of him who sits on the throne and from the wrath of the Lamb!' (Rev. 6:12-15).

The day of our Lord Jesus Christ will be comprehensive in its severity. The New Testament warns us that the final Day of the Lord is yet to come. It warns us that this future day will be universal in scope and comprehensive in its severity. What impact should this knowledge have on how we live our life in the here and now? The apostle Peter addresses this very question in 2 Peter 3:9-10 where he describes the inevitability and destructive power which will accompany the return of Jesus Christ. After describing the nature of that day he moves on to explain how the knowledge of this day should impact the lives of believers in this present age:

> Since everything will be destroyed in this way, what kind of people ought you to be? You ought to live holy and godly lives as you look forward to the day of God and speed its coming. That day will bring about the destruction of the heavens by fire, and the elements will melt in the heat (2 Peter 3:11-12).

Do you see Peter's point here? He is telling us that the knowledge of the Day of the Lord should spur us on to 'live holy and godly lives' in the here and now. He is linking eschatology to ethics. Knowing what is coming should impact how we live now. Why? Because we know that part of the purpose of the Day of the Lord is to rid the world of sin and wickedness. A healthy knowledge and proper fear of the Day of the Lord can play a powerful role in our sanctification.

On the other hand, if we come to deny the Day of the Lord, then apathy and complacency can set in. The prophecy of Zephaniah illustrates this very point. As you will recall from the beginning of this chapter, one of the problems in Judah during Zephaniah's time was that the people had come to think that God was not coming in judgement. They were thinking to themselves, 'The Lord will do nothing, either good or bad' (Zeph. 1:12). They lost sight of God's judgement and they were living unholy and ungodly lives. They thought judgement was not coming for them, but only for the other nations. In the second chapter of Zephaniah's prophecy he sets forth a list of pagan nations which God promises to judge. This list is a veritable 'Who's Who' of the great enemies of Judah: Philistia (2:4-7), Moab and Ammon (2:8-11), Cush (or Ethiopia, 2:12), and Assyria (2:13-15). It is not difficult to imagine that the people of Judah must have been cheering when they heard God pronouncing his judgement against these hated rival nations. However, Judah's cheering must have turned to an eerie silence when Zephaniah began to declare that God's judgement was not just for those nations, but for Judah as well. In the beginning of the third chapter, Zephaniah states that Judah will also be judged for the following reasons:

She obeys no one, she accepts no correction. She does not trust in the LORD, she does not draw near to her God. Her officials are roaring lions, her rulers are evening wolves, who leave nothing for the morning. Her prophets are arrogant; they are treacherous men. Her priests profane the sanctuary and do violence to the law (Zeph. 3:2-4).

Judah had grown complacent. The people did not think God would judge them. Their apathy towards God and their disbelief in his coming judgement contributed to their unholy lives.

The people in Zephaniah's time were living as if there was no coming Day of the Lord. Peter admonishes New Testament believers to live their lives in light of this coming day. How are you living your life? Are you living like Judah? Are you living as if there is no coming Day of Judgement?

The Apostle Paul informs us in 1 Thessalonians that there will be two different reactions to the Day of the Lord. Those who do not believe in a coming Day of Judgement will be caught by surprise: '…for you know very well that the day of the Lord will come like a thief in the night. While people are saying, "Peace and safety", destruction will come on them suddenly, as labor pains on a pregnant woman, and they will not escape' (1 Thess. 5:2-3). However, those who trust in Christ and live in expectation of his return will not be caught off guard: 'But you, brothers, are not in darkness so that this day should surprise you like a thief' (1 Thess. 5:4). This latter group will be spared on that dreadful day: 'For God did not appoint us to suffer wrath but to receive salvation through our Lord Jesus Christ. He died for us so that, whether we are awake or asleep, we may live together with him' (1 Thess. 5:9-10). What will be your reaction to the inevitable coming of the Day of the Lord?

The warnings of Zephaniah regarding the Day of the Lord should not be forgotten or dismissed. For the church is ever at risk of falling into complacency. The church must keep the knowledge of the Day of the Lord ever before it. The modern church and the world around us are both in desperate need of hearing the following warning from Zephaniah:

> Gather together, gather together, O shameful nation, before the appointed time arrives and that day sweeps on like chaff, before the fierce anger of the Lord comes upon you, before the day of the Lord's wrath comes upon you. Seek the LORD, all you humble of the land, you who do what he commands. Seek righteousness, seek humility;

perhaps you will be sheltered on the day of the LORD's anger (Zeph. 2:1-3).

The knowledge of this day not only encourages us to seek righteousness and to live godly lives, but it also reminds us of the importance of making our calling and election sure (1 Peter 1:10). On the Day of the Lord, we want to be found in Christ. As Matthew Henry put it:

> How solicitous should we all be to make our peace with God before the Spirit withdraw from us, or cease to strive with us, before the day of grace be over or the day of life, before our everlasting state shall be determined on the other side of the great gulf fixed! ... It concerns us all to make it sure to ourselves that we shall be hid in the great day of God's wrath...[8]

Jesus is Lord of the coming Day of the Lord. Knowledge of this fact should lead you to ask yourself two questions. First, are you living now in light of the knowledge of this coming day? Is it spurring you on to live a holy and godly life? Second, and more importantly, do you know the Lord of the coming day? Will you be taken by surprise or will you be taken to live with him for ever?

JESUS IS LORD OF THE NEW DAY

The New Testament not only tells us that Jesus is the Lord of the coming Day of Judgement, but it also proclaims that he is Lord of the new day. However, unlike the Day of the Lord, which is a future event related to Christ's second coming, this hopeful new day has already dawned with the first coming of Jesus Christ.

Zephaniah promised that in the new day God's people would be marked by three characteristics: diversity (including people from all nations), humility and holiness. Let's examine how these three characteristics are foretold in Zephaniah's prophecy and fulfilled in the New Testament.

First, Zephaniah promised a diverse church which would include people from all nations. This promise is revealed in the third chapter of Zephaniah's prophecy. In this chapter we learn not only that God's judgement will encompass all nations (Zeph. 3:8, '...I have decided to assemble the nations, to gather the kingdoms and to pour out my wrath on them...'), but also that he promises to redeem people from all nations: 'Then will I purify the lips of the peoples, that all of them may call on the name of the LORD and serve him shoulder to shoulder. From beyond the rivers of Cush my worshipers, my scattered people, will bring me offerings' (Zeph. 3:9-10). Zephaniah 3:9-10 is one of the great Old Testament passages which promised that the church would one day be composed of both Jews and Gentiles. In verse 9 there is a direct reference to a future Gentile inclusion in the phrase, 'Then will I purify *the lips of the peoples*, that *all of them* may call on the name of the Lord...' (emphasis mine).[9] What a tremendous promise, particularly when contrasted with the severity of God's judgement on the nations voiced in verse 8. Raymond Dillard and Tremper Longman, reflecting on the contrast between verses 8 and 9, note, 'He who assembled the nations to hear his judgment (Zeph. 3:8) will also assemble them to receive his grace (v. 9); all will call on the name of the Lord.'[10] Zephaniah promises that Gentiles will be among the people of God. However, we must not overlook verse 10. In this verse we also have a promise that the Jews who would be dispersed in the forthcoming Babylonian invasion would one day be set free to worship God and bring him offerings. What is so amazing about these two verses is that they provide an Old Testament promise of a New Testament reality. Zephaniah promises that a new day is coming when God's church will be a diverse community including both Jews and Gentiles.

The New Testament demonstrates that this new day dawned with the first coming of Jesus Christ. First, the ministry of Jesus led to the destruction of the 'dividing wall of hostility' which separated Jews and Gentiles (Eph. 2:14). Due to the work of Christ, Jews and Gentiles are no longer in conflict, but rather they stand shoulder to shoulder just as Zephaniah promised (Zeph. 3:9-10). Jesus has made it possible for all nations to worship God and call upon his name. The book of Acts unfolds the promise set forth in Zephaniah's prophecy. In Acts chapter 2, dispersed Jews from every nation gathered together to receive the Spirit and hear the good news (Acts 2:5), then this same Spirit and good news was sent out from Jerusalem to the very ends of the earth (Acts 1:8). Furthermore, Zephaniah's promise of a united kingdom of God including both Jews and Gentiles was echoed in the words of the apostle Peter on the Day of Pentecost when he proclaimed, 'The promise is for you and your children and for all who are far off – for all whom the Lord our God will call' (Acts 2:39). In this declaration Peter applies the promises of God to both Jews ('you' in v. 39) and the Gentiles ('all who are far off' in v. 39). The apostle Paul, in his letter to the Ephesians, reminds the Gentiles that they are no longer 'far off', but rather have joined the household of God through the redemptive work of Jesus Christ: 'But now in Christ Jesus you who once were far away have been brought near through the blood of Christ' (Eph. 2:13). Jesus fulfils the promise of Zephaniah 3:9-10; the church is a diverse community consisting of all nations.

Second, Zephaniah promised that the church would one day be marked by humility: 'But I will leave within you the meek and humble, who trust in the name of the LORD' (Zeph. 3:12). This promise was also fulfilled by Jesus Christ, who through his incarnation and life of service set an example of humility for his people to emulate. For example, in Philippians 2, Paul calls on us to follow the example of Jesus by displaying humility in our communities: 'Do nothing out of selfish ambition or vain conceit, but in humility consider others better than yourselves' (Phil. 2:3). In his epistle to the Colossians, Paul calls us to clothe ourselves with humility (Col. 3:12). Likewise, in his epistle to Titus, Paul admonishes Titus to 'Remind the people to be subject to rulers and authorities, to be obedient, to be ready to do whatever is good, to slander no one, to be peaceable and considerate, *and to show true humility toward all men*' (Titus 3:1-2, emphasis mine). Clearly, one of the marks of a Christian is humility. We all know too well that this attribute is not perfected in the Christian in this age, but it is a distinguishing mark of Christ's people.

Finally, Zephaniah promised that one day God's people would possess holiness: 'The remnant of Israel will do no wrong; they will speak no lies, nor will deceit be found in their mouths' (Zeph. 3:13). Jesus Christ has fulfilled this promise by making holiness a distinguishing mark of his people. Yes, Christians continue to struggle with sin, but there has been a definitive change in every true believer.[11] Paul has no qualms in calling believers 'saints' (or 'holy ones'). There is a real sense in which the Christian is free from the dominion of sin in this present age by means of his union with Christ. It is entirely proper to refer to Christians as 'holy' in this age. Paul did exactly this in his greeting to the Colossian church: '*To the holy* and faithful brothers in Christ at Colosse: Grace and peace to you from God our Father' (Col. 1:2, emphasis mine). Again, our holiness is not complete in this age, but it is a distinguishing mark of Christ's people.

The new day has indeed already dawned with the first coming of Christ. However, that new day has not come in its fulness. Christ has not finished saving people from every nation. Christians do not currently display perfect humility, nor do they display perfect holiness in their conduct. The new day has been partially realized in this present age, but much more remains to be fulfilled. There is an 'already' aspect to the new day, but there is also a 'not yet' aspect to it. In this present age we will continue to have trials and sufferings, but God promises that one day he will gather us and bring us home. God speaks of this 'not yet' aspect of the Day of the Lord through his prophet Zephaniah:

'At that time I will deal with all who oppressed you; I will rescue the lame and gather those who have been scattered. I will give them praise and honor in every land where they were put to shame. At that time I will gather you; at that time I will bring you home. I will give you honor and praise among all the peoples of the earth when I restore your fortunes before your very eyes', says the Lord (Zeph. 3:19-20).

In the New Testament Christ reiterates this very promise. He promises that on the Day of the Lord he will come again to bring us home (John 14:2-3) and that through him we will not only have our fortunes restored, but inherit the very kingdom of God: 'He said to me: "It is done. I am the Alpha and the Omega, the Beginning and the End. To him who is thirsty I will give to drink without cost from the spring of the water of life. *He who overcomes will inherit all this, and I will be his God and he will be my son*"' (Rev. 21:6-7, emphasis mine). Therefore, knowing what is to come, Christians should eagerly desire the coming of the Lord so that we might experience the fulness of the new day.

However, our anticipation of the dawning of the new day is not only for our comfort, but it is also meant to work as a stimulus to holiness in this present age. As you will recall from the previous section of this chapter, the apostle Peter calls upon believers to use the knowledge of the coming day of judgement as an incentive to live godly lives in this present age (2 Peter 3:11). Interestingly, in the very same passage, Peter calls upon believers to also use the knowledge of the dawning of the new day for the very same end: 'But in keeping with his promise we are looking forward to a new heaven and a new earth, the home of righteousness. *So then, dear friends, since you are looking forward to this, make every effort to be found spotless, blameless and at peace with him*' (2 Peter 3:13-14, emphasis mine). The knowledge of the coming Day of Judgement and the knowledge of the dawning of the new day are to produce the same effect in Christians, which is godliness. Are you using the knowledge of the coming of the new day in this manner? Are you making every effort to be found spotless and blameless? Are you displaying the humility of Christ? Do you long to be holy as God is holy? Or are you living just like everyone else? Are you just blending into the crowd?

It is interesting to note that the unfaithful leaders in Zephaniah's time enjoyed being 'clad in foreign clothes' (Zeph. 1:8-9). Apparently, they did not want to be recognized as the people of God, but preferred to assimilate the customs of the surrounding unbelieving nations. They wanted to fit in with the rich and the powerful instead of with the people of God. Is this reflective of your attitude? Are you clad in the clothes of your culture or do you endeavour to live your life in light of the knowledge of the imminent return of Jesus Christ? The Bible demands that eschatology impact our ethics in the here and now. Jesus is the Lord of the new day. My question for you is, 'Are you presently serving the Lord of the new day?'

A TALE OF TWO DAYS

Zephaniah tells the tale of two contrasting days, a day of judgement and a day of restoration. Jesus is the Lord of both of these days and your relationship to him will determine how you experience them. If you are not trusting in Christ you will be caught by surprise and you will know the fear and terror of the Day of the Lord. If you are trusting in Christ, then you will experience the joy of the new day. Zephaniah describes this joy at the end of his prophecy:

> Sing, O Daughter of Zion; shout aloud, O Israel! Be glad and rejoice with all your heart, O Daughter of Jerusalem! The LORD has taken away your punishment, he has turned back your enemy. The LORD, the King of Israel, is with you; never again will you fear any harm. On that day they will say to Jerusalem, 'Do not fear, O Zion; do not let your hands hang limp. The LORD your God is with you, he is mighty to save. He will take great delight in you, he will quiet you with his love, he will rejoice over you with singing' (Zeph. 3:14-17).[12]

Make certain that you experience the fulness of joy described by Zephaniah. Make sure that you are serving the Lord of the Day of the Lord. That's how Zephaniah speaks of Jesus.

QUESTIONS FOR DISCUSSION

1. Discuss what role the Day of the Lord should have in evangelistic preaching and outreach.

2. Read 2 Peter 3:10-14 and discuss how the Day of the Lord

should impact our ethics in this age. Make a commitment to use this knowledge as a stimulus to godliness in your own life. Pray about this right now.

3. What attitude does Scripture call us to have regarding the Day of the Lord? See Mark 13:35-37; Luke 12:35-36; 1 Thessalonians 5:1-5 and 2 Peter 3:10.

4. Discuss ways in which modern Christians repeat the sin of those in Zephaniah's day who were 'clad in foreign clothes' (Zeph. 1:8-9). Discuss ways in which Christians can avoid this sin. Can you think of New Testament passages which speak to this issue?

Chapter 10

THE TEMPLE OF GREATER GLORY: HAGGAI

HAVE YOU EVER BEEN DISAPPOINTED? Has someone ever made a promise to you and then failed to fulfil the promise? It is a difficult thing to be disappointed. I can recall the first time I was deceived by advertising. I was about ten years old. I was looking through a comic book and I saw an advertisement for a set of military figurines. The ad was filled with brilliant colours and the figurines were displayed in a variety of action packed poses. I became even more excited when I saw what I could get for my money. The ad promised me that I would receive 500 pieces for a ridiculously low price. I quickly made arrangements to send away for this exciting product. Finally, after what seemed like an exorbitant amount of time, the long awaited package came to my door. I was a bit shocked at first because the package was much smaller than I had anticipated. It did not seem like it could hold the 500 action packed figurines displayed in the ad. I assumed it must have been a partial shipment and I tore open the box with great vigour. However, my excitement quickly turned to disappointment as my eyes beheld the contents of the box. The little box did contain 500 pieces, but they were incredibly small and certainly not action packed. They did not look anything like the advertisement. I had moved from excited expectation to discouraged disappointment.

A similar thing happened to the people of God during the time of Haggai. They were filled with anticipation after being delivered from exile in Babylon. They were excited by the prospect of a restored Jerusalem and a new Temple. They believed they could recapture their former glory as a nation. When they returned to Jerusalem, however, they quickly became disappointed at the reality of what they saw. This disappointment soon led to discouragement and eventually, to apathy. The people simply gave up. Haggai came to challenge and encourage the people of God by calling them to fix their eyes on the future hope of the coming Messiah.

ENTERING INTO HAGGAI'S WORLD

We know very little about Haggai's background. The book of Haggai simply refers to him as 'the prophet', giving no indication of his background or ancestry (Hag. 1:1). We do know, however, that he was a contemporary of Zechariah and that his name is related to a Hebrew word for 'feast' or 'festival'.[1] We also know that he prophesied after the Babylonian exile. The Babylonian exile began in 586 B.C. when the Babylonians conquered Judah, deported the Jews and destroyed Jerusalem and the Temple. In 538 B.C., the Persian king, Cyrus, issued a decree permitting the Jews to return to Jerusalem. Haggai was sent to prophesy to this post-exilic community, a community which was now free to rebuild Jerusalem, rebuild the Temple, worship God and start over again.

However, the Babylonian invasion and subsequent captivity exacted a heavy toll on Judah. For example, when the people returned to Jerusalem they were small in number, around 50,000.[2] They also came back to a Jerusalem in shambles. Furthermore, they faced opposition from other nations, particularly their long-time rivals the Samaritans.[3] Finally, they faced economic hardship. Their economy and national wealth was utterly depleted as a result of the captivity and exile. In the face of these obstacles, the people of Judah quickly moved from excitement to discouragement. Their discouragement became so great that within two short years after receiving their freedom they suspended their efforts to rebuild the temple. For sixteen years, from 536 B.C. to 520 B.C., Judah ceased to make any progress on the house of God. It was into this setting that God sent Haggai.

Haggai personally bridges the gap between the pre-exilic and post-exilic prophets. He likely experienced the Babylonian invasion, likely lived as an exile in Babylon, likely returned with Judah from exile, and likely participated in the initial efforts to rebuild the temple. By 520 B.C., when Haggai commenced his four month ministry, he was an old man. He had seen much in his time and God chose him as his messenger to wake up his slumbering people.

THE PROPHET'S MESSAGE: CHALLENGE AND ENCOURAGEMENT

Haggai's message was two-fold. First, he challenged the people to resume their efforts to rebuild God's house. Second, he encouraged them by promising them a future filled with glory, a glory which would surpass anything they could imagine. Let's begin by looking at the first part of Haggai's message, his challenge to Judah.

Four times in his prophecy Haggai uses the phrase 'Give careful thought to your ways' (1:5, 1:7, 2:15 & 2:18). By means of this phrase, the prophet was challenging the people to re-examine their priorities. The people had become discouraged in their efforts to rebuild the Temple and they were assuaging their consciences by attributing their failure to God's providence. They used the following excuse to justify their unfaithfulness: 'The time has not yet come for the LORD house to be built' (Hag. 1:2). In essence they were saying, 'Well, in God's providence, it just isn't the right time to build the Temple.' This false piety allowed them to pursue other priorities like their own homes, lives and interests. Willem VanGemeren described Judah's priorities at this time as follows: 'They were preoccupied with making a living, improving their standard of life, rationalizing their adversities, and accusing the Lord of being untrue to his promises.'[4]

It is important to remember that the Temple was not ancillary to Old Testament religion. It was required to administer the sacrificial system mandated by God's law. The people of Judah, however, were too busy with their own needs to be bothered with the house of God. So Haggai called them on it: 'Is it a time for you yourselves to be living in your paneled houses, while this house remains a ruin?' (Hag. 1:4). Haggai called on the people to change their priorities. He told them to seek first the kingdom of God. He told them to get to work on God's house: 'This is what the LORD Almighty says: "Give careful thought to your ways. Go up into the mountains and bring down timber and build the house, so that I may take pleasure in it and be honored", says the LORD' (Hag. 1:7-8).

Haggai's challenge was penetrating and direct, but he also brought great encouragement to the people of God. He gave them three promises regarding their future. First, he promised them that they could be strong because God was with them in their task: '"But now be strong, O Zerubbabel", declares the LORD. "Be strong, O Joshua son of Jehozadak, the high priest. Be strong, all you people of the land", declares the LORD, "and work. For I am with you", declares the LORD Almighty' (Hag. 2:4). The task before the people was indeed great. They faced real obstacles in their efforts to build the Temple. It was a difficult task. They truly lacked resources. They really faced opposition. However, God promised them they could be strong because he was with them in the task.

Second, God promised them that he is sovereign over all of creation, including the nations around Judah: 'This is what the LORD Almighty says: "In a little while I will once more shake the heavens and the earth, the sea and the dry land. I will shake all nations, and the desired of all nations will come, and I will fill this house with glory", says the LORD Almighty' (Hag. 2:6-7). Remember, Judah was facing opposition from other nations and God promised them he was in control of these nations. He was telling them that these enemy nations were unable to thwart his plan. In fact, implied in this promise is the idea that these enemy nations would one day become willing participants in God's economy.

Third, God promised them that their future would be more glorious than their past: "'The glory of this present house will be greater than the glory of the former house", says the LORD Almighty. "And in this place I will grant peace", declares the LORD Almighty' (Hag. 2:9). God told them that a more glorious Temple was coming and that in that Temple he would grant peace to his people.

By means of these three encouraging promises Haggai turned the eyes of the people away from the discouragement of the present to the hope of a glorious future. Unlike my childhood experience, in which I was promised one thing and received another, God fulfilled these promises in a way that went far beyond anything that the people of Judah could imagine in their time, for these three promises were ultimately fulfilled in the person and work of Jesus Christ. This is how Haggai turns our eyes to Jesus.

JESUS IS OUR STRENGTH: HE IS WITH US

Through the prophet Haggai, God promised his people that they could be strong because he would be with them. He promised them that he would be with them through the adversities which would confront them as they built the Temple. When God encouraged the people to be strong, this phrase would have sparked in their minds God's faithfulness to his people in the past. Moses spoke similar words of encouragement to the entire nation after informing them that he would be unable to enter the Promised Land with them. He told them to be 'strong and courageous' (Deut. 31:6). Likewise, God told Joshua to 'be strong and courageous' after he assumed the role of leader of the people of Israel (Josh. 1:6). Similarly, David gave this charge to Solomon as he ascended the throne of Israel (1 Chr. 28:20). Furthermore, on each of these occasions the encouragement to be strong was followed by the promise of God's presence. For example, Moses told Israel that they could be strong because 'the LORDyour God goes with you; he will never leave you nor forsake you' (Deut. 31:6). God told Joshua he could be strong because 'No one will be able to stand up against you all the days of your life. As I was with Moses, so I will be with you; I will never leave you nor forsake you' (Josh. 1:5). David told Solomon he could be strong because 'the LORD God, my God, is with you. He will not fail you or forsake you until all the work for the service of the temple of the LORD is finished' (1 Chr. 28:20). The Bible teaches us that our ability to be strong is linked with God's presence with us.

This linkage continues in the New Testament and it is particularly focused on the presence of our Lord Jesus Christ. In several places, the apostle Paul calls upon new covenant believers to be strong:

> • 'Finally, be strong in the Lord and in his mighty power' (Eph. 6:10).
> • 'Be on your guard; stand firm in the faith; be men of courage; be strong' (1 Cor. 16:13).
> • Paul encouraged Timothy with these words: 'You then, my son, be strong in the grace that is in Christ Jesus' (2 Tim. 2:1).

Just as it was in the time of Haggai, we too can be strong only because Jesus promises to be with us. Paul experienced this dynamic in his own life. In 2 Timothy 4:17 he noted, 'But the Lord *stood at my side* and gave me strength' (emphasis mine). When Paul went to Macedonia, he was viciously opposed by the Jews and he became fearful. Then Jesus came to him and told him in a vision, 'Do not be afraid; keep on speaking, do not be silent. *For I am with you*, and no one is going to attack and harm you, because I have many people in this city' (Acts 18:9-10, emphasis mine). This promise, however, is not just for Paul. Jesus promises to be with every one of us: 'And surely I am with you always, to the very end of the age' (Matt. 28:20). He will never leave us nor forsake us (Heb. 13:5). We can be strong because he is with us! In fact, we can be strong not only because of his presence, but because Jesus is the very source of our strength. The apostle Paul, who faced many trials, relied upon the strength of Christ and not his own strength. Repeatedly in his letters Paul declared that Jesus was the source of his strength. Note how Paul attributes his strength to Christ in the following examples:

- 'I can do everything through him *who gives me strength*' (Phil. 4:13, emphasis mine).
- 'I thank Christ Jesus our Lord, *who has given me strength*' (1 Tim. 1:12, emphasis mine).
- 'But the Lord stood at my side and *gave me strength*' (2 Tim. 4:17, emphasis mine).

In order to make it through the discouragements and trials of this age, we must remember that Jesus promises to be with us and that he will be the source of our strength!

JESUS IS SOVEREIGN OVER ALL

In the time of Haggai, God also encouraged the people by reminding them that he is sovereign over all things. He expressed his sovereignty and power by promising to one day shake the heavens, earth, sea, dry land and the nations (Hag. 2:6-7). At the heart of this promise was the notion that God's people would prevail because he is in control of all things. God would shake everything else, but his people would not be shaken. In the New Testament we learn that these words spoken through the prophet Haggai will be ultimately fulfilled at the return of Jesus Christ.

In the letter to the Hebrews, the author encourages his people to persevere through the trials and travails of this present age. He calls on them to be strong and to not shrink back. He admonishes them to look forward to the return of Jesus Christ. The author of Hebrews draws on the prophecy of Haggai to remind the people that Jesus controls all things and that he will deliver them when he returns:

At that time his voice shook the earth, but now he has promised, 'Once more I will shake not only the earth but also the heavens.' The words 'once more' indicate the removing of what can be shaken – that is created things – so that what cannot be shaken may remain. Therefore, since we are receiving a kingdom that cannot be shaken, let us be thankful, and so worship God acceptably with reverence and awe, for our 'God is a consuming fire' (Heb. 12:26-29).

The writer to the Hebrews informs us that when Jesus returns the entire created order will be shaken just as Haggai promised, but we will not be shaken because we are subjects of the kingdom of Christ! Jesus promises us that he is sovereign over all things.

Included in God's promise of sovereignty over all things was his promise that he is sovereign over the nations. He was telling the people that the nations would not only cease interfering with the plan of God, but one day they would become willing participants in that plan. This promise of the nations one day serving God is powerfully expressed in Haggai 2:7 when God states that the 'desired of nations will come' to God's house. Historically, this phrase was often considered as a direct reference to Jesus Christ, that he is the 'desired of all nations'. However, this verse is probably not a direct reference to Jesus.[5] I think the best way to interpret this passage is to see it as a promise that one day people from all nations will come to worship God at his Temple. The New Testament confirms that through Jesus this promise was fulfilled. The New Testament tells us that elect from every nation are part of his kingdom: 'And they sang a new song: "You are worthy to take the scroll and to open its seals, because you were slain, and *with your blood you purchased men for God from every tribe and language and people and nation*"' (Rev. 5:9, emphasis mine). Jesus promises us that he is sovereign over all nations.

Jesus is the Greater Glory

In the days of Haggai, God also promised that the Temple they were in the process of building would one day be of greater glory than the Temple which was destroyed by the Babylonians (Hag. 2:9). This was an astounding promise because the first Temple was a magnificent sight to behold. This second Temple they were constructing paled in comparison to the first. The book of Ezra tells us that the people who had seen the former Temple wept aloud when the foundation for the second Temple was laid (Ezra 3:12-13). The people could tell from the nature of the foundation that this Temple would be structurally inferior to the former Temple. God recognized what the people were thinking and he spoke directly to this issue in Haggai's prophecy by inquiring of the people, 'Who of you is left who saw this house in its former glory? How does it look to you now? Does it not seem to you like nothing?' (Hag. 2:3). It did indeed seem to them like nothing in comparison to the first Temple. Structurally speaking, there was no comparison. The first was more glorious by far. However, God promised that this second Temple would one day be of greater glory than the first. Was this promise ever fulfilled?

Some suggest that Haggai's prophecy was fulfilled by the work of Herod. In fact, Herod did adorn the second Temple for his own glory. He made it a magnificent physical structure. This is evidenced in the New Testament by the testimony of one of the disciples as he gazed at Herod's temple: 'As he was leaving the temple, one of his disciples said to him, "Look, Teacher! What massive stones! What magnificent buildings!"' (Mark 13:1). However, I don't believe that God's promise of a temple of greater glory was fulfilled by the work of the wicked King Herod.[6] In fact, I don't think God was ultimately referring to a temple of stone. Rather, I think he was referring to the One in whom all the fulness of Deity lived in bodily form (Col. 2:9). The apostle John informs us that in Jesus the fulness of God's glory dwelled: 'The Word became flesh and made his dwelling among us. We have seen his glory, the glory of the One and Only, who came from the Father, full of grace and truth' (John 1:14). The structural second Temple foreshadowed the dwelling of the living God with his people through the greater temple of the incarnate Son of God! Jesus makes this very connection between his body and the temple in John 2:18-21:

> Then the Jews demanded of him, 'What miraculous sign can you show us to prove your authority to do all this?' Jesus answered them, 'Destroy this temple, and I will raise it again in three days.' The Jews replied, 'It has taken forty-six years to build this temple, and you are going to raise it in three days?' *But the temple he had spoken of was his body* (emphasis mine).

With the coming of Jesus, the temple of greater glory, a physical temple is no longer needed. What could possibly surpass the glory of Jesus Christ? As John Calvin put it:

> ...for though they were to gather the treasures of a thousand worlds into one mass, such a glory would yet be corruptible; but when God the Father appeared in the person of his own Son, he then glorified indeed his Temple; and his majesty shone forth so much that there was nothing wanting to a complete perfection.[7]

The Apostle John tells us that in the age to come the city will not require a temple because the Lamb will be the temple (Rev. 21:22). It is through Jesus that this prophecy of Haggai is fulfilled! A temple of greater glory has come! Jesus made this very point to the Jews: 'I tell you that one greater than the temple is here' (Matt. 12:6).

Furthermore, the greater glory of Jesus is seen not only in the fact that his body was the temple of God, but also in the fact that he builds his people into a spiritual temple, a temple characterized by peace. The people in Haggai's day were called to build a temple and God promised them that in that place he would grant his 'peace' (Hag. 2:9). The New Testament links these dual themes of temple building and peacemaking to the work of Jesus Christ. The New Testament reveals that Jesus is not only the temple, but the temple builder. It also reveals that Jesus not only brought peace to his people by reconciling them to God (Col. 1:19-20 and 1 Tim. 2:5-6), but also by tearing down the wall of conflict between Jews and Gentiles. In his epistle to the Ephesians, Paul reveals this greater glory of Christ's which is expressed in his peacemaking and temple-building work. Note how Paul weaves together these twin themes in the following passage from Ephesians:

> *For he himself is our peace*, who has made the two one and has destroyed the barrier, the dividing wall of hostility, by abolishing in his flesh the law with its commandments and regulations. His purpose was to create in himself one new man out of the two, *thus making peace*, and in this one body to reconcile both of them to God through the cross, by which he put to death their hostility. *He came and preached peace* to you who were far away *and peace to those who were near*. For through him we both have access to the Father by one Spirit. Consequently, you are no longer foreigners and aliens, but fellow citizens with God's people and *members of God's household, built on the foundation* of the apostles and prophets, with Christ Jesus himself *as the chief cornerstone. In him the whole building is joined together and rises to become a holy temple in the Lord. And in him you too are being built together to become a dwelling in which God lives by his Spirit* (Eph. 2:11-22, emphasis mine).

Now that's a glorious temple! The people in Haggai's day were longing for a temple of greater glory, a place where God would grant his peace. The New Testament tells us that this longing was fulfilled in Jesus Christ, the temple of greater glory!

Clearly, there is a great deal of comfort in the message of Haggai. He assures us that we can be strong in Jesus, that Jesus is sovereign over all, that he is the temple of greater glory and the that he is the builder of a spiritual temple of peace. However, it's important that we do not lose sight of the challenge contained in Haggai's prophecy. His message included challenge as well as comfort. Remember, he called upon the people of God to examine their priorities and to give careful thought to their ways. Haggai issued this challenge because the people of Judah were not making their relationship with God of paramount importance. Rather, they were striving and striving to prosper themselves at the expense of their religious life. It is interesting to note that although Judah made their own prosperity central, God did not allow them to succeed. Notice what Haggai tells them about all their efforts to enhance their own wealth: 'You have planted much, but have harvested little. You eat, but never have enough. You drink, but never have your fill. You put on clothes, but are not warm. You earn wages, only to put them in a purse with holes in it' (Hag. 1:6). Haggai pointed out to them the futility of setting their own prosperity above their relationship with God. This challenge is extremely relevant for our own day. After all, does not the description of Judah's striving in Haggai 1:6 aptly describe the spirit of our own age?

Western culture is consumed with striving after material prosperity at all costs. We live in an ever striving culture, a treadmill culture where we never seem to obtain the prize. James Montgomery Boice noted the relevance of Haggai 1:6 for our own age, stating, 'I do not know of any passage in the Bible that better describes the feverish yet ineffective activity of our own age.'[8] It is important to remember that Christians are not immune to this problem. This problem is not just a problem in the wider culture; it is a problem in our churches as well. Christians too easily assimilate into the norms of our consumer culture. We too often put material prosperity over our relationship with God. We too often neglect giving to the Lord's work and attempt to assuage our consciences with religious platitudes. Often our churches are in shambles, both physically and spiritually, while our homes are finely decorated. Haggai calls you to examine your priorities. As you go down the list of priorities in life, where does God's house rank? Where do your church commitments rank? Most importantly, where does your relationship with Jesus Christ rank? Is Jesus Christ the central priority in your life? If not, Haggai calls on you to 'Give careful thought to your ways'.

THE GREAT PROMISE KEEPER

This chapter began with a story of my boyhood disappointment. I was promised one thing and received another. Perhaps you have experienced the pain of a broken promise. Perhaps someone vowed to love you until death only to desert you when things became difficult. Perhaps you were promised a job for life, only to receive a termination notice. Our lives are full of disappointments. People often break their promises. However, Haggai reminds us that God never breaks a promise and never disappoints us. This is as true now as it was in Haggai's time. Be assured and comforted by the fact that Jesus will never disappoint you. He will never promise you one thing and give you another. There is no 'bait and switch' advertising in the kingdom of God. The temple of greater glory has come in Jesus Christ just as God promised. That's how Haggai speaks of Jesus.

QUESTIONS FOR DISCUSSION

1. As you will recall from the chapter, Old Testament scholar Willem VanGemeren described Judah's priorities at the beginning of Haggai's ministry as follows: 'They were preoccupied with making a living, improving their standard of life, rationalizing their adversities, and accusing the Lord of being untrue to his promises.'[9] Discuss how our modern church and culture reflect similar priorities. Discuss ways in which you must reprioritize your life.

2. One of the criticisms which Haggai levelled against the people of God in his day was their unwillingness to give their time and money to the work of the church. Discuss whether you think the modern church faces similar challenges and discuss how these problems can be addressed.

3. We have learned in this chapter not only that Jesus is the temple of greater glory, but that he is including each one of us as stones in that temple (1 Peter 2:5). Read 1 Corinthians 6:15-20 and discuss the ethical implications of being part of the temple of Christ. Discuss how this truth must impact the way we conduct our lives as Christians.

4. Read Haggai 1:6 and discuss whether you think this is an accurate description of our own culture. Also discuss ways by which Christians can avoid getting caught in the same type of lifestyle.

Chapter 11

LOOKING BACK AND LOOKING FORWARD: ZECHARIAH

WINSTON CHURCHILL ONCE REMARKED, 'The longer you look back, the farther you can look forward.'[1] One of the distinguishing marks of humanity is our ability to preserve our history and learn from it. If we fail to remember and learn from our history, then we are likely to repeat the mistakes of the past. However, we can also become so imprisoned by our history that we never move forward. We must maintain a proper balance between the past and the future. Zechariah's prophecy deals with this very issue. He called on the people of God to look back and learn from their painful history, but he also called upon them to look forward to their glorious future, a future dominated by the work of the Messiah.

ENTERING INTO ZECHARIAH'S WORLD

Zechariah, like Haggai, was a post-exilic prophet. He prophesied in the latter part of the sixth century B.C. A second similarity between Zechariah and Haggai is that they both were concerned with the nation's effort to rebuild the Temple. Although we know very little about Zechariah personally, there is good reason to believe that he was from a priestly family.[2] His prophecy is the longest among the Minor Prophets. It is not, however, an easy prophecy to comprehend. The church father Jerome referred to Zechariah as the 'most obscure' book in the Hebrew Scriptures.[3] Zechariah's prophecy is difficult to understand because it is filled with visions and symbolic imagery. Given this symbolic nature, it should not surprise us that the prophecy was a major source for the symbolism which appears in the book of Revelation.[4] In addition to its influence on the book of Revelation, Zechariah is also significant to New Testament theology because it is the most frequently cited Old Testament book in the passion narratives[5] of the Gospels.[6] It is difficult to overstate the influence of Zechariah's prophecy on the New Testament. For example, Walter Kaiser has noted that there are seventy-one quotations or allusions to Zechariah in the New Testament, one third of which occur in the Gospels and nearly another third of which occur in the book of Revelation.[7]

Zechariah's prophecy breaks neatly into two parts. The first eight chapters deal with the problems of the past, the concerns of the present and the hopes of the immediate future. Essentially, the first part of Zechariah's prophecy is oriented to needs and hopes of the restored post-exilic community. Zechariah addressed these needs and hopes through a series of night visions. The purpose of these visions was primarily to assure the post-exilic community of God's faithfulness. Willem VanGemeren has noted: 'The visions, like John's in the Apocalypse, were given for the purpose of comfort that the godly might know that the Lord was zealously working out all aspects of redemption.'[8] The last six chapters (9-14) have a very different focus. These final chapters look forward into the future. They are filled with eschatological and apocalyptic symbolism and imagery which is expressed through prophetic oracles or sermons. The two sections of Zechariah's prophecy also differ with regards to the main characters described in them. The first part refers to known historical figures such as Joshua the high priest and Zerubbabel the civil leader. In the second part the main character is an unidentified and unnamed shepherd.

In Zechariah's time the people of God were beginning a new day. They were back in their homeland and they were free. Their future, however, was unclear. Would they return to the sins which resulted in their forefathers entering into captivity or would their future be marked by fidelity to God? Would they be able to re-build the Temple? Would they be protected from their enemies? The people were at a crossroads. They needed to be challenged regarding their past and encouraged regarding their future. It was into this setting that God sent Zechariah, and he came to Judah with a two-fold message. He told them to look back with discernment and look forward with reassurance.

THE PROPHET'S MESSAGE: LOOK BACK AND LOOK FORWARD

Zechariah began his prophecy with a stern warning about the past. His name means 'remember' and that's exactly what he called on the people to do. He called them to remember their painful past. His purpose in this was to ensure that they would not repeat the errors of their forefathers which had resulted in the Babylonian captivity. He reminded them that the captivity occurred because 'The LORD was very angry with your forefathers' (Zech. 1:2). He warned them not to repeat the sins of the past: 'Do not be like your forefathers' (Zech. 1:4). He then reminded them what would occur if they repeated the sins of the past. He did this by asking them a simple rhetorical question: 'Where are your forefathers now?' (Zech. 1:5). Do you see Zechariah's point here? He was warning the people that if they repeated the sins of the past they would end up like their forefathers, many of whom suffered and died in the Babylonian invasion and subsequent captivity. A generation was lost due to unfaithfulness to God. Zechariah did not want the people to repeat the mistakes of the past, so he admonished them in a direct, personal and painful way. Zechariah's prophecy began with a call to look back, to remember the past with the hope that it would not be repeated. However, Zechariah's prophecy quickly moves into dealing with the present struggles and challenges of the post-exilic community.

Beginning in verse 7 of the first chapter, Zechariah begins to address the challenges facing the post-exilic community through a series of night visions. The imagery of these visions is vivid and multi-faceted. The visions include images such as multi-coloured horses, a wall of fire and a flying scroll. While a detailed interpretation of the meaning of each of these eight visions is beyond the scope of this book, it is helpful for our purposes to recognize the main themes.[9] What unites these visions is that they all deal with threats to the well-being and success of the post-exilic community. They reveal that there are two major enemies which threaten to destroy the community. First, there are external enemies. The surrounding pagan nations are threatening to invade and destroy the people of God. This threat is particularly apparent in the second (1:18-21) and third (2:1-13) visions. The other major threat comes from within the community. The visions reveal that the community can also come to destruction through its own internal sinfulness and disobedience to God. This threat is most starkly revealed in the sixth vision (5:1-4) and the seventh vision (5:5-11).

However, these visions also provide great comfort for the post-exilic community regarding their future because they assure the people that these two threats will not prevail. First, Zechariah assures the people that God will prevail over the nations. The main thrust of the first vision (1:7-17) and the eighth vision (6:1-8) is the vengeance of God against the nations who persecute his people. Second, Zechariah assures the people that their own sins will be dealt with in the two middle visions. In the fourth vision (3:1-10), Joshua, the high priest, is depicted in filthy garments which represent his sinfulness. Satan is standing before Joshua and accusing him regarding his sins. But this is not just about the sinfulness of the high priest; rather it speaks of the sinfulness of the entire nation, because the high priest functioned as a representative of the nation. In this vision God replaces the filthy garments of the priest with clean robes of righteousness. God promises to deliver the people from their sins. Furthermore, the fifth vision (4:1-14) depicts seven lamps which have a limitless supply of fuel and wicks that are never extinguished. This is a promise that God will be faithful in preserving the work of his Temple. Remember, in the old covenant the Temple was the place where a believer would come for provisional atonement for his sins. Normally, the priest would have to fill the lamps and change the wicks twice a day, but this vision promises that it is God who will keep the lamps burning. The promise to the people is that they won't lose their place of worship and atonement.

While the night visions of Zechariah provide great comfort about the future, they pale in comparison to the pronouncements of the last section of Zechariah's prophecy (Zech. 9-14). In these final chapters, Zechariah reveals that a deliverer is coming – a deliverer who is a shepherd, priest and king. After admonishing the people to remember their painful past and encouraging them to face the challenges of the present, Zechariah turns their eyes to a vision of their glorious future, a future dominated by the work of the Messiah.

By means of his night visions and prophetic oracles, Zechariah ultimately turns the eyes of the people, and our eyes, to Jesus. It is Jesus who ultimately delivers the people of God from their internal and external enemies. It is Jesus who deals with our past and holds our future. Zechariah reminds us that Jesus has dealt with our past by removing our sins and paying the penalty for them. He also reminds us that Jesus holds our future because he is our king.

Jesus Has Dealt with Our Past

As we have seen, Zechariah began his prophecy by calling on the people not to repeat the sins of their forefathers. He began with the problem of their past. Of course, we know that the Jews did, in fact, repeat the sins of their forefathers. They would once again enter into unfaithfulness, as we will see in the following chapter regarding the prophecy of Malachi. Why did they not learn from their past? The answer is the same for them as it is for us, for this is not just an Old Testament problem. This is a human problem. This is *our* problem. The explanation for the continual cycle of unfaithfulness in their lives, and in ours, is the problem of sin. Every human being is born into this world with a past. We carry a legacy from our first parents Adam and Eve. We are born sinners. Zechariah revealed that this basic human problem would be addressed by the coming Messiah. The prophet informs us that the Messiah came to deal with our past, a past which stretches all the way back to the Garden of Eden. The Messiah dealt with our past by removing our sins and paying the penalty for them.

This glorious Messianic work is foretold powerfully in the amazing and dramatic scene in the third chapter of Zechariah's prophecy. As mentioned previously, the scene involves Joshua, the high priest, dressed in filthy clothes and under attack by Satan who has come to accuse him. The Angel of Lord intervenes to defend Joshua and rebuke Satan. The Angel of the Lord then commands that Joshua's filthy clothes be exchanged for a set of clean clothes. He explains to Joshua that this exchange of garments is a metaphor for the forgiveness of sins: 'See, I have taken away your sin, and I will put rich garments on you' (Zech. 3:4). Do you see what is going on here? Joshua is the high priest, the representative of the people to God, but he is defiled. He is covered with utter filth.[10] God makes it clear that this filth represents his sinfulness. However, the Angel of the Lord promises to give Joshua clean garments and by doing so he promises to remove his sin. This is an amazing vision of forgiveness! However, it is just the beginning.

As chapter three progresses, the vision becomes even more amazing. Not only will Joshua's personal sin be dealt with, but God will also deal with the sins of those whom Joshua represents. In Zechariah 3:8-9, God promises that he will deal with the sins of all his people:

> 'Listen, O high priest Joshua and your associates seated before you, who are men symbolic of things to come: I am going to bring my servant, the Branch. See, the stone

I have set in front of Joshua! There are seven eyes on that one stone, and I will engrave an inscription on it', says the LORD Almighty, *'and I will remove the sin of this land in a single day'*, (Zech. 3:8-9, emphasis mine).

What a glorious promise! God will deal with our sins by sending his 'servant, the Branch'. Who is being identified in these verses as the one who was coming to remove the sins of his people? It is none other than the Lord Jesus Christ!

The third chapter of Zechariah predicts the coming of Jesus by employing two Messianic titles: 'servant' and 'Branch'. The prophet Isaiah declared that the Messiah would bear the title of 'servant':

Here is *my servant*, whom I uphold, my chosen one in whom I delight; I will put my Spirit on him and he will bring justice to the nations. He will not shout or cry out, or raise his voice in the streets. A bruised reed he will not break, and a smoldering wick he will not snuff out. In faithfulness he will bring forth justice, (Isa. 42:1-3, emphasis mine).[11]

The New Testament clearly links the language of this text to the work of Jesus Christ. In fact, Matthew declares that this very prophecy of Isaiah was fulfilled by Jesus Christ (Matt. 12:17-18). Jesus is the servant of God the Father who comes to fulfil the Father's plan. He comes to remove our sins.

The prophet Isaiah also revealed that the Messiah would bear the title of 'Branch'. For example, in Isaiah 11:1 the prophet declared, 'A shoot will come up from the stump of Jesse; from his roots a *Branch* will bear fruit' (emphasis mine). This title goes back to the Davidic covenant. As you will recall, Jesse was the father of King David (1 Sam. 16:1). In 2 Samuel 23:5 David states, 'Is not my house right with God? Has he not made with me an everlasting covenant, arranged and secured in every part? Will he not *bring to fruition* my salvation and grant me my every desire?' (emphasis mine). The Hebrew word which is translated by the phrase 'bring to fruition' is an agricultural word which carries the ideas of causing to grow, sprouting or branching out. David was promised that his kingly dynasty would be everlasting. He was promised that from his lineage would branch forth an eternal king. The New Testament declares that Jesus is the 'Son of David' (Matt. 1:1) and the 'Offspring of David' (Rev. 22:16). Jesus is the branch which came forth from the stump of Jesse; he is the promised Messiah who removes our sins.

In addition to the titles of servant and branch, there may be a third reference to the Messiah in this chapter. In verse 9 God states that he will place a 'stone' in front of Joshua and on this stone God will engrave the inscription, 'and I will remove the sin of this land in a single day'. Although there is not universal agreement on this point, many commentators interpret the 'stone' here as a reference to the Messiah. In support of this connection is the fact that the Messiah is referred to as a stone in Psalm 118:22 and in 1 Peter 2:4-8.[12] What makes this connection all the more convincing is the fact that the stone in Zechariah 3:9 bears the following inscription: 'and I will remove the sin of this land in a single day'. Isn't this a summary of the redemptive work of Christ? Isn't he the one who removed the sins of his people in one day?

The glorious truth taught in the third chapter of Zechariah is that Jesus has dealt with our past. He has removed our sin. He is our Great High Priest who, unlike the high priest Joshua, is sinless and undefiled. Furthermore, unlike the priests of the Old Testament, Jesus dealt with our sin in one full swoop, once and for all, in one single day! Hebrews 10:12 states of Jesus, 'But when this priest had offered for all time one sacrifice for sins, he sat down at the right hand of God.' Jesus has dealt with our past by removing our sins.

A significant part of Christ's work in removing our sins was his paying the penalty for them. He did this through his suffering in his earthly life and death. Zechariah's prophecy is unique among the Minor Prophets in that he revealed that suffering would be part of the Messiah's work. Zechariah proclaimed that the Messiah would suffer by being rejected, pierced and smitten.

First, in chapter 11 of Zechariah's prophecy, the prophet is called upon by God to assume the role of the shepherd of God's people. Zechariah attempted to fulfil this task, but he was ultimately rejected by the people. By rejecting Zechariah as their shepherd the people were ultimately also rejecting God who sent him. To add insult to injury, the people dismissed Zechariah from his duties as a shepherd with the payment of the paltry sum of thirty pieces of silver. [13] This exchange is recorded in Zechariah 11:12-13:

> I told them, 'If you think it best, give me my pay; but if not, keep it.' So they paid me thirty pieces of silver. And the LORD said to me, 'Throw it to the potter' – the handsome price at which they priced me! So I took the thirty pieces of silver and threw them into the house of the LORD to the potter (Zech. 11:12-13).

When God described this payment as a 'handsome price' this was a display of outrage and sarcasm, not approval. The people had rejected the shepherd and the one who sent him. The New Testament confirms that Zechariah was describing the rejection of Jesus. The Gospel accounts confirm that the Good Shepherd was rejected by his people for the paltry sum of thirty pieces of silver (Matt. 26:15, 27:6-9). Zechariah informs us that the Messiah would suffer by being rejected.

Secondly, Zechariah revealed that the Messiah would suffer by being pierced:

> And I will pour out on the house of David and the inhabitants of Jerusalem a spirit of grace and supplication. They will look on me, the one they have pierced, and they will mourn for him as one mourns for an only child, and grieve bitterly for him as one grieves for a firstborn son (Zech. 12:10).

Here the prophet proclaimed that the Messiah would come to Jerusalem proclaiming grace, but his people would crucify him.

The New Testament confirms that Zechariah was speaking of the crucifixion of Jesus: 'Instead, one of the soldiers *pierced Jesus' side* with a spear, bringing a sudden flow of blood and water ... These things happened so that the scripture would be fulfilled: "Not one of his bones will be broken", and, as another scripture says, "They will look on the one they have pierced"' (John 19:34, 36-37, emphasis mine). After his death, just as Zechariah predicted, the people mourned for him: 'When all the people who had gathered to witness this sight saw what took place, they beat their breasts and went away' (Luke 23:48). Zechariah revealed that the Messiah would suffer by being pierced.

Third, and finally, Zechariah foretold that the Messiah would suffer by being smitten by his own Father: '"Awake, O sword, against my shepherd, against the man who is close to me!" declares the LORD Almighty. "Strike the shepherd, and the sheep will be scattered, and I will turn my hand against the little ones"' (Zech. 13:7). It is clear from this text that God the Father is wielding the sword and that it is his shepherd, 'the man who is close' to him, the one who is his companion, who will be smitten. The Old Testament scholar, C.F. Keil, contended that the phrase 'the man who is close to me' (or as Keil translates it 'nearest one' or 'fellow') clearly connects this prophecy to the Messiah:

> The idea of nearest one (or fellow) involves not only similarity in vocation, but community of physical or spiritual descent, according to which he whom God calls His neighbour cannot be a mere man, but can only be one who participates in the divine nature, or is essentially divine. The shepherd of Jehovah, whom the sword is to smite, is therefore no other than the Messiah...[14]

Zechariah proclaimed that the Messiah would suffer by being smitten by his own Father.[15] Once again, the New Testament connects the prophecy of Zechariah to the crucifixion of Jesus. After the Last Supper, Jesus told his disciples: 'This very night you will all fall away on account of me, for it is written: "I will strike the shepherd, and the sheep of the flock will be scattered'" (Matt. 26:31).

Zechariah's description of the suffering Messiah begs the question: 'Why must the Messiah suffer?' Think about it for a moment. Why would the Father smite his shepherd? Why would he smite 'the man who is close' to him? The Messiah committed no fault, and yet he was rejected, pierced and smitten. Why? The only way to make sense of the suffering of the Messiah is by understanding that the Messiah became our sin bearer. Isaiah makes this very connection in his prophecy: 'But he was pierced for our transgressions, he was crushed for our iniquities; the punishment that brought us peace was upon him, and by his wounds we are healed' (Isa. 53:5).[16] Jesus was rejected, pierced and smitten, to pay the penalty for our sins.

I began this section by noting that every human being is born into this world with a legacy from Adam and Eve. Our problem is that we are sinners. Zechariah proclaimed that this basic human problem would be addressed by the coming Messiah. The good news is that the Messiah has come. Jesus has come and he has dealt with our legacy of sin. He has removed our sins and he has paid the penalty for them. This fact allows us to look back on our sinful history in an entirely new light.

When we look back on our sinful past as Christians, it is for the purpose of seeing the liberating work of Jesus Christ in our lives. We look back to remember how Jesus has redeemed us from sin. It is important to emphasize the fact that we have been liberated from our sinful past by Jesus Christ, because some Christians are haunted by the severity and consequences of their past sins. The weight of their past sinfulness can often become so heavy that they end up in deep depression over their past. They end up as prisoners of their past. Dr Martyn Lloyd-Jones noted that this is one of the causes of spiritual depression. He advised those who have this particular type of spiritual depression to:

Never look back again; never waste your time in the present; never waste your energy; forget the past and rejoice in the fact that you are what you are by the grace of God, and that in the Divine alchemy of His marvelous grace you may yet have the greatest surprise of your life and existence and find that even in your case it will come to pass that the last shall be first. Praise God for the fact that you are what you are, and that you are in the Kingdom.[17]

Jesus came to deliver us from our past sinfulness, not to imprison us in that state. He doesn't save us from our sin only to bring it up against us again and again. Jesus has delivered us from our past. He has put our sins far from us: 'as far as the east is from the west, so far has he removed our transgressions from us' (Ps. 103:12). Due to the work of Jesus Christ we can look back on our past and rejoice.

JESUS HOLDS OUR FUTURE

Although Zechariah's prophecy begins by looking back, it is predominately about looking forward. The point of this forward-looking emphasis was to encourage the people of God about their future, to remind them that God is in control of the future and that he will bring his promises to fulfilment. Zechariah's prophecy revealed that this glorious future would be ushered in, administrated and transformed by a coming king.

In the previous section we saw how Jesus dealt with our past by removing our sins and suffering the penalty for them. This task was accomplished by Jesus through his priestly role. However, the prophecy of Zechariah also revealed that the coming Messiah would not only be a priest, but a king as well:

Tell him this is what the LORD Almighty says: 'Here is the man whose name is the Branch, and he will branch out from his place and build the temple of the LORD. It is he who will build the temple of the LORD, and he will be clothed with majesty and will sit and rule on his throne.

And he will be a priest on his throne. And there will be harmony between the two' (Zech. 6:12-13, emphasis mine).

These verses revealed that the Messiah would be a priest-king. He would bring harmony between these two offices which were so often in conflict in the Old Testament. Zechariah promised a coming ruler, but what would his rule be like?

Zechariah answers this question in chapter 9 of his prophecy. Zechariah 9:9-10 describes the nature of his rule as follows:

Rejoice greatly, O Daughter of Zion! Shout, Daughter of Jerusalem! See, your king comes to you, righteous and having salvation, gentle and riding on a donkey, on a colt, the foal of a donkey. I will take away the chariots from Ephraim and the war-horses from Jerusalem, and the battle bow will be broken. He will proclaim peace to the nations. His rule will extend from sea to sea and from the River to the ends of the earth (Zech. 9:9-10).

His rule would be marked by righteousness and peace. He would not come riding a war horse, but he would come on a lowly donkey. He was not coming to conquer through brute force, but to make peace through the cross (Col. 1:20).[18] His rule would be all-encompassing; it 'will extend from sea to sea' and it would be transforming. It would control the future of the world. This transforming power of his rule is brought out in numerous other parts of Zechariah's prophecy as Willem VanGemeren so aptly notes:

He is the Priest-King who serves 'the Lord of all the earth' (4:14) and rules over all who believe on him, Jews and Gentiles (8:20-23) … In the end, the Messiah will establish the kingdom of God on earth. He will vindicate the saints and judge the unbelieving nations: 'On that day his feet will stand on the Mount of Olives … Then the Lord my God will come, and all the holy ones with him'

(14:4-5). On that glorious day the Lord and Creator of humankind will transform everything (14:6-8) and grant his blessings on the new community, which may share in this transformed and holy world (14:20-21).[19]

Zechariah predicted a coming king who would control and transform the future of the world. The New Testament confirms that this king has come in Jesus Christ:

The next day the great crowd that had come for the Feast heard that Jesus was on his way to Jerusalem. They took palm branches and went out to meet him, shouting, 'Hosanna!' 'Blessed is he who comes in the name of the Lord!' 'Blessed is the King of Israel!' Jesus found a young donkey and sat upon it, as it is written, 'Do not be afraid, O Daughter of Zion; see, your king is coming, seated on a donkey's colt' (John 12:12-15).[20]

Jesus is the king described by Zechariah. Jesus is the king who controls and transforms our future.

Zechariah called on the people to be encouraged by looking forward to this glorious future, a future controlled and transformed by the reign of the Messiah. Although the reign of Jesus has already commenced, Christians today continue to look forward to our glorious future which will be transformed by Christ. We look forward to his return. We look forward to the end of suffering and sin. We look forward to the consummation of all things. We look forward to our heavenly home. We look forward to being with Christ and being like Christ. We have so much to look forward to and we know it will come to pass because Jesus holds our future.

It is important to remind ourselves of the fact that Jesus holds the future because Christians often become fearful of their futures. Much of my pastoral counselling is really dealing with people's fear of the future. Sometimes this fear can become crippling to a Christian's walk. Fear of the future can lead us into spiritual depression just as much as being consumed in sorrow over our past sinfulness. Dr. Marytn Lloyd-Jones identified fear of the future as another of the causes of spiritual depression and he advises us that we can avoid the fear by focusing on the work of Jesus Christ in our lives:

> Instead of allowing the future and thoughts of it to grip you, talk to yourself, remind yourself of who you are and what you are, and of what Spirit is within you; and, having reminded yourself of the character of the Spirit, you will be able to go steadily forward, fearing nothing, living in the present, ready for the future, with one desire only, to glorify Him who gave His all for you.[21]

Note how much Lloyd-Jones emphasizes the centrality of the Spirit's work in providing us reassurance regarding the future. The present indwelling of the Spirit is vital to a Christian's ability to face the future. After all the Spirit is given to believers as a counsellor to be with us for ever (John 14:16). This reassuring work of the Spirit is also revealed in Zechariah's prophecy. In chapter 4 Zerubbabel, the civil ruler of Israel, is facing significant challenges in rebuilding the Temple and God comforts his servant with these words of reassurance: 'So he said to me, "This is the word of the LORD to Zerubbabel: 'Not by might nor by power, *but by my Spirit*', says the LORD Almighty"' (Zech. 4:6, emphasis mine). God told Zerubbabel that he could face the future because God would enable him to overcome through his Spirit. Jesus makes the same promise to believers in the New Testament. He told his disciples that he would not leave them orphans (John 14:18), but rather he would be with them through his Holy Spirit. Jesus promised to send a comforter to his people to help them face the challenges of the future. In fact, it is this present indwelling of the Spirit which enables believers to be reassured about the certainty of their future in Christ. This is why the apostle Paul speaks of the giving of the Holy Spirit as 'a deposit guaranteeing our inheritance' (Eph. 1:14). We need not have any fear in looking forward to our future because the Spirit of Christ dwells in us. Jesus holds our future and through him we will overcome!

LOOKING BACK AND LOOKING FORWARD

Perhaps you are haunted by your past or are fearful of your future. The only way to be liberated from these burdens is by understanding your past and future in relation to your union with Jesus Christ. In Jesus, you can rejoice in your past because you can see how he has dealt with your past, how he removed your sins and paid the entire penalty for them. In Jesus, you can also rejoice in the prospect of your future because you know it is he who holds your future. You know that he is your great king. In Jesus Christ, we can both look back and forward with utter joy. That's how Zechariah speaks of Jesus.

QUESTIONS FOR DISCUSSION

1. Often Christians are trapped by their past because they are unable to believe that God can really forgive them of their past sinfulness. On the other hand, sometimes Christians fail to learn from their past and repeat the same mistakes. Zechariah's prophecy calls us to have an awareness of our past. Discuss how our past can be used effectively in our Christian life. Discuss how it can be used to edify and encourage others. Discuss how it can be used in evangelistic outreach.

2. Make a list of your concerns about the future. After making the list, read Philippians 4:6-7 and take some time to pray about these matters.

3. The last chapter of Zechariah's prophecy speaks of the glorious restoration which will be brought about by the Messiah. Read Zechariah 14:9 and discuss how this text relates to the following Scriptures: Deuteronomy 6:4 and Philippians 2:4. What do these texts reveal to us about the nature and work of Jesus Christ?

4. In Zechariah's time, the civil ruler, Zerubbabel faced tremendous obstacles. In Zechariah 4:6, God told him he would overcome these obstacles through the power of his Spirit. Read Zechariah 4:6 and discuss its implications for how you live the Christian life. Compare and discuss these New Testament texts: John 14:26 and 16:13; Romans 8:1-16; and Galatians 5:16-25.

Chapter 12

GETTING THE MESSAGE: MALACHI

HAVE YOU EVER ATTEMPTED TO COMMUNICATE a message to someone and they just didn't get it? Perhaps you have tried to correct
someone's behaviour, but your point was just not getting through
to them. Often we attempt to communicate messages to others by
subtle means. My wife, for example, often employs subtle tactics
with me. When I have neglected some husbandly duty, she usu-
ally leaves me some type of sign which is intended to subtly remind me that I had better get to work. Let me give you an example
of this. As I mentioned in a previous chapter, my wife and I are
currently in the process of an international adoption and she has
been carefully decorating the nursery over the past several months
in anticipation of our coming child. While she is in charge of
most of the decorating process, I was assigned the duty of assem-

bling the crib which was stored in the basement. Over the past few weeks I have noticed that the parts of the disassembled crib have made their way from the basement to the nursery. This is a subtle message that I am supposed to be doing something! Needless to say, I got the message.

Most of us prefer to use a subtle approach when attempting to correct others. Sometimes, however, the subtle method of communication is not successful and a more direct approach is required. Often people won't listen until they are jolted by direct and repeated admonishment. God is rarely subtle when he communicates his message to us. This is certainly the case with the prophecy of Malachi. Malachi directly challenged the people of God to repent of their sins before it was too late. He called on them to get his message and to get it right away!

ENTERING INTO MALACHI'S WORLD
Malachi prophesied in the early part of the fifth century B.C. The Babylonian exile was quickly becoming a distant memory, the Temple had been rebuilt and the people of God were returning to a level of normalcy. As you will recall, the other post-exilic prophets, Haggai and Zechariah, gave the people a glorious vision of the future. However, by the time of Malachi, this glorious future had not yet been realized and the people began to question God's love and veracity. They began to lose faith in God and this lack of faith was manifested in their behaviour. In Malachi's day, infidelity was rampant among the clergy and the people. It was into this setting that God sent Malachi.

THE PROPHET'S MESSAGE
Malachi's name means 'my messenger' and that's exactly what he was. He was God's messenger sent to challenge the people of God to believe in him and live according to his commandments. Malachi's job was to point out to the people of God the areas in which they were being unfaithful. Malachi informed the people that there were four major areas of unfaithfulness. He told them they were unfaithful in worship, they had an unfaithful clergy,

they were unfaithful in their marriages, and finally, they were unfaithful in their financial giving to God's work.

First, they were unfaithful in worship. This unfaithfulness was displayed in the quality of the sacrifices they brought to God. Note God's words in Malachi 1:13: '"And you say, 'What a burden!' and you sniff at it contemptuously", says the LORD Almighty. "When you bring injured, crippled or diseased animals and offer them as sacrifices, should I accept them from your hands?" says the LORD.' God's law required the people to bring the best of their flocks, but they were bringing their worst. They were bringing injured, crippled and diseased animals.

Secondly, they had an unfaithful clergy. The clergy demonstrated their unfaithfulness through their lack of personal piety and by teaching false doctrine. In Malachi 2:6-7, God describes what a priest ought to be:

> True instruction was in his mouth and nothing false was found on his lips. He walked with me in peace and uprightness, and turned many from sin. 'For the lips of a priest ought to preserve knowledge, and from his mouth men should seek instruction – because he is the messenger of the LORD Almighty' (Mal. 2:6-7).

God stated that a priest ought to walk in 'peace and uprightness' and provide 'true instruction'. However, in Malachi's day the priests were failing on both counts: '"But you have turned from the way and by your teaching have caused many to stumble; you have violated the covenant with Levi", says the LORD Almighty' (Mal. 2:8). The priests were not leading people into righteousness by their piety and preaching, but rather they were causing them to stumble.

Third, they were also being unfaithful in their marriages. One manifestation of this infidelity in marriage was their practice of marrying unbelieving wives: 'Judah has broken faith. A detestable thing has been committed in Israel and in Jerusalem: Judah has desecrated the sanctuary the LORD loves, by marrying the daughter of a foreign god' (Mal. 2:11). A second manifestation of their unfaithfulness in marriage was the widespread practice of divorce:

> Has not the LORD made them one? In flesh and spirit they are his. And why one? Because he was seeking godly offspring. So guard yourself in your spirit, and do not break faith with the wife of your youth. 'I hate divorce', says the LORD God of Israel ... (Mal. 2:15-16).

Unfaithfulness had taken root, not only in worship and the clergy, but in the most intimate of all human relationships. The people were unfaithful in their marriages.

Fourth, the people were displaying their unfaithfulness by failing to render to God their tithes and offerings: 'Will a man rob God? Yet you rob me. But you ask, "How do we rob you?" In tithes and offerings. You are under a curse – the whole nation of you – because you are robbing me' (Mal. 3:8-9). The people were unfaithful in their giving.

Clearly, God's message to his people was not subtle. He sent Malachi to directly confront and admonish the people regarding their unfaithfulness in these four areas. Amazingly, however, the people failed to get the message. Their failure to get the message is evidenced by their responses to God when he confronted them with these specific charges.

For example, when God charged them with defiling him through their unfaithful worship, they responded by saying, 'How have we defiled you?' (Mal. 1:7). When God charged the clergy with showing contempt for his name, they responded by saying, 'How have we shown contempt for your name?' (Mal. 1:6). When God charged them with robbing him through their unfaithful financial giving, they responded by saying, 'How do we rob you?' (Mal. 3:8). They denied and disputed nearly every charge, and if this was not bad enough, they went a step further and denied God's love for them as well. When God expressed his love for them they retorted, 'How have you loved us?' (Mal. 1:2). Do you see the audacity of the people of God? They are breaking God's commandments left and right and they say to God, 'How have you loved us!' They didn't see the unfaithfulness in their own lives, but rather they accused God of unfaithfulness in his lack of love for them. They just didn't get the message.

The people in Malachi's time failed to get God's message that they needed to repent of their sin and turn to serve him, so God promised to send other messengers. It is by this promise that Malachi turns our eyes to Jesus.

Jesus is the Ultimate Messenger

The book of Malachi revealed that God would send a series of messengers to his people to call them to repentance. First, there was Malachi himself. As we have seen, his name means 'my messenger' and he came to call God's people to repentance. However, in Malachi 3:1 the prophet speaks of another messenger who will be sent by God: 'See, I will send *my messenger*, who will prepare the way before me' (emphasis mine). This promise is echoed in Malachi 4:5: 'See, I will send you the prophet Elijah before that great and dreadful day of the LORD comes.' The New Testament confirms that this promised messenger was John the Baptist (Luke 1:17). Like Malachi, John the Baptist came to call the people of God to repentance: 'In those days John the Baptist came, preaching in the Desert of Judea and saying, "*Repent*, for the kingdom of heaven is near"' (Matt. 3:1-2, emphasis mine). Two messengers, Malachi and John the Baptist, both proclaimed the same message: 'Repent!'

Malachi, however, speaks of a third messenger in the second part of Malachi 3:1: '"Then suddenly the LORD you are seeking will come to his temple; *the messenger of the covenant*, whom you desire, will come", says the LORD Almighty' (emphasis mine). This third messenger is none other than the Messiah, the Lord Jesus Christ.

There are three reasons to conclude that Jesus is the one referred to as 'the messenger of the covenant' in Malachi 3:1. First, Malachi declares that the 'Lord' is coming to his Temple. The title 'Lord' excludes the possibility that this coming messenger is a human prophet. He is *the Lord* and he is coming to *his* Temple. Second, there are two different Hebrew words used which are translated as 'Lord' in this passage. If you look this verse up in your Bible, you will note that the first appearance of the word 'Lord' is in lower case letters and the second appearance of 'LORD' is displayed in upper case letters. The first appearance of the word 'Lord' is a translation of the Hebrew word *Adon*. The second appearance of the word 'LORD' is a translation of the Hebrew word *Yahweh*. Why are these two different words employed in this text? I believe it is for the purpose of distinguishing the redemptive work of the Father and Son. I believe the text is telling us that God the Father (denoted by the name *Yahweh*) promised to send God the Son (denoted by the name *Adon*) to his people.[1] Finally, I believe that Jesus is being spoken of here because the title given to this coming one is 'the messenger of the covenant'. The Bible tells us that Jesus alone is the mediator of God's covenant with his people, and therefore, he must be the one identified by the phrase 'the messenger of the covenant'.[2] This title for Jesus, 'the messenger of the covenant', is so glorious that it requires some additional reflection before we continue.

By attributing to Jesus the title 'the messenger of the covenant', God is stating that Jesus alone is the Lord of his gracious covenant dealings with his people. We learn that Jesus is the central figure in God's divine dealings with his people in both testaments of Scripture. Walter C. Kaiser, after connecting the phrase 'the messenger of the covenant' to Jesus Christ, marvellously expounds on the vast redemptive scope of the meaning of this phrase:

> The covenant referred to here is the single plan of God contained in the succession of covenants that began with the word issued to Eve in Genesis 3:15, continued in the word given to Shem in 9:27, to Abraham in 12:2-3, to David in 2 Samuel 7:12-19, and renewed and enlarged in Jeremiah 31:31-34. This messenger of the covenant is the same person God sent ahead of Israel as they left Egypt (Exod. 23:20-23), in whom Yahweh placed his own

name (23:31). There can be no mistaking his identity, for to equate the name of God with his angel or messenger is to call him divine! Elsewhere this messenger is called 'the Angel of the Lord', which is also understood to be a preincarnate appearance of Christ, or a Christophany (Exod. 33:14-15; Judg. 6:12; Isa. 63:9). *The Messiah is the mediator of all the covenants of the Bible (Heb. 8:8-13; 12:24); he is the communicator, executor, administrator, and consummator of that divine plan* (emphasis mine).[3]

The phrase 'the messenger of the covenant' reveals the glory and centrality of the work of Jesus Christ in the plan of redemption.

As we have seen, Malachi informs us that Jesus is the third, final and ultimate messenger sent to God's people. Like those who preceded him, he came with a message of repentance: 'From that time on Jesus began to preach, "Repent, for the kingdom of heaven is near"' (Matt. 4:17). Three messengers all proclaiming the same message: 'Repent!' The question for us is whether we are getting this message. The problems raised in Malachi's prophecy are not foreign to us. They are perennial problems. In fact, when the final messenger came he confronted the people on the four areas raised in Malachi's prophecy. Jesus called on the people to worship God in 'spirit and in truth' (John 4:24) while chastising the Pharisees for worshipping him in vain (Matt. 15:9). He continually pointed out the unfaithfulness of the clergy, particularly of the Pharisees and the teachers of the law (Matt. 23:15-30). He denounced the frivolous exercise of divorce and admonished them regarding the true purpose of marriage (Mark 10:2-9). He instructed them on the true nature of giving (Luke 21:1-4) while attacking them for turning God's house into a den of robbers (Matt. 21:12).

Unfaithfulness was a problem in Malachi's day, it was a problem at the time of Jesus' earthly ministry and it remains a problem for us today. The Bible continues to call on Christians today to repent of these very same sins. These sins remain with us. Think about it for a moment. Isn't the modern church suffering from unfaithfulness in her worship and clergy? Isn't the modern church suffering from unfaithful marriages and unfaithful stewardship? Are these not our problems? Are not the sins described in Malachi the sins which continue to plague the evangelical church in our day?

Consider the area of worship. Don't you often bring God less than your best in worship? The New Testament commands you to bring God your 'sacrifice of praise – the fruit of lips that confess his name' (Heb. 13:15). Are you bringing him your best sacrifice? Do you prepare yourself to worship him? Do you care how late you stay out on Saturday evening? Do you pray for the preacher and the preaching of the Word during the week? Do you ask the Holy Spirit to use worship to strengthen you and bless your family? Are you faithful in attending worship?

How about the problem of an unfaithful clergy? Isn't this a massive problem in the modern church? It would be easy for me to attack those who have denied the inspiration of Scripture, the deity of Christ, or those who are ordaining homosexuals to the ministry. However, let me bring this a bit closer to home. Unfaithfulness in the ministry is not just a problem in the liberal wing of the church. Remember, God stated in Malachi that a good priest has two qualities: personal piety and faithfulness in teaching. The New Testament confirms this two-fold standard through Paul's instruction to Timothy: 'Don't let anyone look down on you because you are young, *but set an example for the believers in speech, in life, in love, in faith and in purity. Until I come, devote yourself to the public reading of Scripture, to preaching and to teaching*' (1 Tim. 4:12-13, emphasis mine). How many of our modern pastors are living up to this standard? How many see their role as flirting with theological novelty rather than preserving God's knowledge? How many cause others to stumble because of their own lack of piety?

Think about the area of marriage. How many of our young people are marrying unbelieving spouses? How many of them think living together before marriage is an acceptable practice? Regarding divorce, statistics show that the church is not much better than the world in this area. Are you instructing your children to marry in the Lord? Are you being faithful to your marital vows?

Finally, consider the area of financial stewardship. The Bible teaches us that God owns everything in our world (Ps. 24:1), but it also teaches us that God calls upon his people to manage or 'steward' his creation. For example, although Adam did not own the Garden of Eden, God called upon him to cultivate it, tend it and keep it (Gen. 2:15). Likewise, God is the true owner of all the wealth we possess and he calls upon us to manage this wealth in accordance with his principles. Stewardship is the practice of managing our wealth in accordance with biblical principles. The people of God in Malachi's time were not acting as good stewards of the wealth which they possessed. They chose to rob God of his tithes. They violated biblical principles of stewardship, particularly in the area of giving to God's church, and God pronounced judgement on them for this failure.

How are you doing in the area of financial stewardship? Christians are commanded to give to God's church and the New Testament standard for giving is extremely high. We are commanded to give regularly (1 Cor. 16:2), cheerfully (2 Cor. 9:7) and liberally (2 Cor. 8:3). Are you living up to this standard or are you robbing God? Do you regularly give to the Lord's work? Our unfaithfulness in giving is crippling the church. How many pastors are underpaid because of our woeful commitment to giving? How many churches are in disrepair because we are robbing God? Remember the warning of Paul: 'Remember this: Whoever sows sparingly will also reap sparingly, and whoever sows generously will also reap generously' (2 Cor. 9:6). Doesn't that describe the modern church? Are we not reaping sparingly? Malachi tells us that if we are faithful in our giving then God will 'throw open the floodgates of heaven and pour out so much blessing that you will not have room enough for it' (Mal. 3:10). Is the church presently experiencing a flood or a drought of God's blessing?

God sent three messengers: Malachi, John the Baptist and the Lord Jesus Christ. What unites these messengers is that they each sounded forth a clarion call to the people of God to repent. The question for you is: 'Are you getting the message?'

JESUS IS THE ULTIMATE MESSAGE

In the previous section, I noted what united Malachi, John the Baptist and Jesus Christ. They were all messengers and they all proclaimed the message of repentance. However, what sets the ministry of Jesus apart from the other two messengers is that he not only came to point out the problem of sin, but also to provide the solution. Jesus was not only the messenger, but also the message.

Malachi promised that the coming Messiah would deal with the problem of sin. For example, Malachi 3:2 states that the 'messenger of the covenant' is coming to purify his people: 'For he will be like a refiner's fire or a launderer's soap'. Two metaphors, refining and laundering, are used here to describe the work of the Messiah. What do these two activities have in common? What is the similarity between the work of a refiner and the work of a launderer? They both purify and cleanse without destroying the underlying substance. The promise here is that Jesus will come to purify and cleanse his people from unfaithfulness.[4]

The New Testament confirms that Jesus is the one who purifies us and cleanses us. John tells us that Jesus purifies us from sin: 'But if we walk in the light, as he is in the light, we have fellowship with one another, and the blood of Jesus, his Son, *purifies us* from all sin' (1 John 1:7, emphasis mine). Paul tells us that Jesus cleanses his church from sin by washing her: '...Christ loved the church and gave himself up for her to make her holy, cleansing her by the *washing* with water through the word, and to present her to himself as a radiant church, *without stain or wrinkle or any other blemish, but holy and blameless*' (Eph. 5:25-27, emphasis mine). Jesus does not come to consume and destroy us, but rather he comes to make us holy. He removes our dross and washes away our stains! Jesus is not only the messenger, but he is also the very message itself!

Malachi informs us that the ultimate message is Jesus Christ and that how you respond to this ultimate message will determine your fate. The prophet drives this point home in the fourth chapter of his prophecy. In this chapter Malachi reveals that the 'great and dreadful day of the Lord' (Mal. 4:6) is coming. It began with the first coming of Christ, but, as we saw in the chapter on Zephaniah's prophecy, it will be fully consummated at his second coming. Malachi tells us that on the great and dreadful day of the Lord Jesus Christ there will be only two categories of people. First, there will be the arrogant and the evildoer who will be consumed by fire (Mal. 4:1). Second, there will be those who trust in Jesus Christ who will be completely liberated: 'But for you who revere my name, the sun of righteousness will rise with healing in its wings. And you will go out and leap like calves released from the stall' (Mal. 4:2). The message of Malachi is that Jesus has come to purify us, cleanse us and set us free from our sins. To reject this message is to reject all hope of redemption. Jesus is the ultimate message, a message which must not be ignored.

GETTING THE MESSAGE

I began this chapter by noting how sometimes we fail to 'get the message'. Often this occurs because the one sending the message is unclear in communicating it. This never happens when God speaks to us. God is never unclear. The Bible is his living message to the world and in it he communicates clearly to us regarding Jesus Christ. In his word, he tells the world that there is only one way to avoid the judgement to come and that is to repent and believe in Jesus Christ. This message cannot be stated more clearly than it is in John 3:16: 'For God so loved the world that he gave his one and only Son, that whoever believes in him shall not perish but have eternal life.' The question for you is: 'Are you getting the message?' That's how Malachi speaks of Jesus.

QUESTIONS FOR DISCUSSION

1. The people in Malachi's time were bringing injured, crippled and diseased animals as their offerings to God (Mal. 1:13). God's command to them, and to us, is to bring him our best in worship (Heb. 13:15). Discuss some ways in which Christians today repeat the mistakes of the people in Malachi's time by bringing less than their best to God in worship.

2. Read the description of a true and faithful priest in Malachi 2:6-7. Discuss how this applies to our church leaders (pastors and elders) in the New Covenant. What qualities should we look for in our leaders according to this text? Can you identify New Testament texts which teach similar principles?

3. The people in Malachi's time were desecrating the institution of marriage (Mal. 2:11, 15-16). Discuss some ways in which marriage is being desecrated in the modern church and in our culture.

4. The people in Malachi's time were also unfaithful in their stewardship of their resources (Mal. 3:8-9). Discuss the biblical concept of stewardship using the following texts as a guide for your discussion: 1 Corinthians 16:2; 2 Corinthians 8:3 and 9:6-7. Can you identify other New Testament texts which address this issue? If so, discuss those texts as well.

NOTES

INTRODUCTION

1. At this time in Israel's history the kingdom was divided. The northern kingdom was called Israel and consisted of ten of the twelve tribes. The southern kingdom was called Judah and included the remaining two tribes. Included in Judah's territory was the city of Jerusalem where the Temple was located. Most of the Minor Prophets deal with Judah because the northern kingdom of Israel was essentially destroyed in 722 B.C. by the Assyrians.

2. Sidney Greidanus, *Preaching Christ from the Old Testament* (Grand Rapids, MI: Eerdmans, 1999), 70.

3. The preacher was Charles Spurgeon (See Greidanus, 158). This demonstrates that even great preachers can fall into this error.

4. I am indebted to the work of Sidney Greidanus on this topic. See Sidney Greidanus, *Preaching Christ from the Old Testament* (Grand Rap-

ids, MI: Eerdmans, 1999), 177-277.

5. The word 'pattern' is the English translation of the Greek word *tupos* from which we get our English word 'type'.

6. At this point you may be wondering what distinguishes typology from the allegorical method which I denounced earlier. After all, both emphasize making connections between the two testaments. The answer to this question is multi-faceted, but the primary difference between the allegorical method and the typological method is that the typological method seeks to make biblically defendable connections between the Old and New Testaments, whereas the allegorical method relies upon the imagination of the interpreter to make unwarranted connections. For a full discussion of the difference between the typological and allegorical methods, and for rules guiding the typological method, see Louis Berkhof, *Principles of Biblical Interpretation* (Grand Rapids, MI: Baker, 1950) pgs. 144-145 and Michael Williams, *The Prophet and His Message* (Phillipsburg, NJ: P & R, 2003, pgs. 124-130.

7. I. Howard Marshall, "An Assessment of Recent Developments," *It Is Written: Scripture Citing Scripture.* ed. D.A. Carson, et. al. (Cambridge: Cambridge Univeristy Press, 1988), 16.

8. Greidanus, 223.

9. John R.W. Stott, *Between Two Worlds: The Art of Preaching in the Twentieth Century* (Grand Rapids, MI: Eerdmans, 1982), 325 as quoted in Greidanus, 259.

CHAPTER 1

1. John Calvin, *Calvin's Commentaries*, vol. 13, trans. Thomas Myers (Grand Rapids, MI: Baker Books, 1989), 43.

2. William Hendriksen, *New Testament Commentary: Exposition of the Gospel According to Matthew* (Grand Rapids, MI: Baker Books, 1995), 130.

CHAPTER 2

1. Charles Dickens, *A Christmas Carol* (Uhrichsville, OH: Barbour Publishing, Inc., 1997), 4.

2. John Murray, *Redemption Accomplished and Applied* (Grand Rapids, MI: Eerdmans, 1955), 114.

3. Sinclair Ferguson notes the connection between the Spirit's work at creation and at Pentecost: 'The "sound like the blowing of a violent wind" echoes the imagery of the powerful operation of the ruach elohim of creation (Gn. 1:2), suggesting that the event about to take place marks the beginning of a new world order.' See Sinclair Ferguson, *The*

Holy Spirit (Downers Grove, IL: IVP, 1996), 60.

4. Ferguson, 37.

5. Westminster Confession of Faith 15:2. One of the proof texts for this section of the Confession is Joel 2:12-13.

6. This motivation for repentance is also expressed by Joel in 2:32 and 3:16-21.

7. Robert Shaw, *An Exposition of the Westminster Confession of Faith* (Great Britain: Christian Focus Publications, 1998), 201.

CHAPTER 3

1. C.S. Lewis, *The Lion, The Witch and The Wardrobe* (New York, NY: Harper Collins, 1978), 200.

2. For a discussion of Amos' social status see Raymond B. Dillard and Tremper Longman's *An Introduction to the Old Testament* (Grand Rapids, MI: Zondervan, 1994), 376.

3. Willem VanGemeren, *Interpreting the Prophetic Word* (Grand Rapids, MI: Zondervan, 1990), 134.

4. Lewis, 180.

CHAPTER 4

1. John Owen, *An Exposition of the Epistle to the Hebrews*, vol. 7 (Carlisle, PA: Banner of Truth, 1991), 298.

2. Vern S. Poythress, *The Returning King: A Guide to The Book of Revelation* (Phillipsburg, NJ: P & R, 2000), 136.

3. Poythress, 136.

4. John Calvin, *Calvin's Commentaries*, vol. 14, trans. Thomas Myers (Grand Rapids, MI: Baker Books, 1989), 452. See also pages 454-455.

CHAPTER 5

1. John Newton, *Out of the Depths* (Grand Rapids, MI: Kregel, 1990).

2. Interestingly, one of Newton's captains made a connection between Newton and the prophet Jonah. He told Newton that his presence made him think he had a 'Jonah on board'. John Newton, *Out of the Depths* (Grand Rapids, MI: Kregel, 1990), 65-66.

3. The sailors displayed their belief by praying to God (Jonah 1:14), offering him sacrifices and making vows to him (Jonah 1:16).

4. Willem VanGemeren, *Interpreting the Prophetic Word* (Grand Rapids, MI: Zondervan, 1990), 149.

5. See also Romans 1:7, 2 Corinthians 1:2, Galatians 1:3, Ephesians 1:2, Philippians 1:2, 1 Thessalonians 1:1, 2 Thessalonians 1:2, 1 Timothy 1:2, 2 Timothy 1:2, Titus 1:4, and Philemon 1:3.

6. See also Galatians 6:18, 1 Thessalonians 5:28, and 2 Thessalonians 3:18.

7. O. Palmer Robertson, *Jonah: A Study in Compassion* (Carlisle, Pennsylvania: Banner of Truth, 1990), 36.

8. As quoted in R. Kent Hughes, *1001 Great Stories & Quotes* (Wheaton, IL: Tyndale, 1998), 190.

CHAPTER 6

1. God displayed his justice by keeping the requirement of two witnesses as prescribed in Deuteronomy 17:6: 'On the testimony of two or three witnesses a man shall be put to death, but no one shall be put to death on the testimony of only one witness.'

2. John Calvin, *Calvin's Commentaries*, vol. 14, trans. Thomas Myers (Grand Rapids, MI: Baker Books, 1989), 338.

3. In Luke 9:31, Jesus speaks with Elijah and Moses regarding his 'departure, which he was about to bring to fulfillment at Jerusalem'. The English word 'departure' is the translation of the Greek word *exodon*. Therefore, Jesus spoke of his crucifixion in Jerusalem as an exodus event.

4. This text may be referring to a particular woman giving birth or to a nation giving birth. I believe it is the former. It is important to remember that Micah would have been familiar with the following prophecy from Isaiah: 'Therefore the Lord himself will give you a sign: The virgin will be with child and will give birth to a son, and will call him Immanuel', (Isaiah 7:14). Either way one interprets it, however, the import of the prophecy is essentially the same. Micah speaks of a future birth of a ruler who will change the world!

5. Willem VanGemeren, *Interpreting the Prophetic Word* (Grand Rapids, MI: Zondervan, 1990), 154.

6. John Calvin, *Calvin's Commentaries*, vol. 14, trans. Thomas Myers (Grand Rapids, MI: Baker Books, 1989), 343.

7. C.F. Keil and F. Delitzsch, *Commentary on the Old Testament: Minor Prophets*, vol. 10 (Peabody, MA: Hendrickson, 1996), 336.

8. Matthew Henry, *Matthew Henry's Commentary on the Whole Bible*, vol. 4 (Peabody, MA: Hendrickson, 1991), 1047.

9. William Hendriksen, *New Testament Commentary: Exposition*

of the Gospel According to Matthew (Grand Rapids, MI: Baker Books, 1995), 831.

10. A very similar exchange occurs in the Gospel of Luke. See Luke 10:25-28.

11. The interpretation of Matthew 5:17 varies among conservative biblical commentators. Some think Jesus was solely referring to his teaching role, that he was fulfilling the law by revealing its full meaning. Others think that Jesus was referring to the fact that he would fulfill the law by keeping it, by living a perfectly righteous life (his so-called 'active obedience'). The two are not mutually exclusive and I believe both are taught in this text.

12. Robert Haldane, *Commentary on Romans* (Grand Rapids, MI: Kregel, 1988), 334.

13. John Calvin, *Calvin's Commentaries*, vol. 14, trans. Thomas Myers (Grand Rapids, MI: Baker Books, 1989), 338.

CHAPTER 7

1. Jonathan Edwards, *Jonathan Edwards on Knowing Christ* (Carlisle, PA: Banner of Truth, 1990), 191.

2. Very similar imagery is used by the psalmist in Psalm 18:8-10.

3. Willem VanGemeren, *Interpreting the Prophetic Word* (Grand Rapids, MI: Zondervan, 1990), 166.

4. As quoted in R. Kent Hughes, *1001 Great Stories & Quotes* (Wheaton, IL: Tyndale, 1998), 189.

5. Some theologians and commentators believe that there is a double fulfillment of this 'cloud coming' of Christ. They contend that the first fulfillment of Matthew 24:30 occurred in 70 A.D. when Jerusalmen and the Temple were destroyed by the Romans. This view, known as 'partial preterism', also contends that the ultimate fulfillment of this text will be realized in the final coming of the Lord on the Last Great Day. According to the parital preterist view, Jesus came as a divine warrior in 70 A.D. to elminiate the old covenant form of worship and clear the way for the fullness of his kingdom. For further study of this partial preterist view see R.C. Sproul, *The Last Days According to Jesus* (Grand Rapids, MI: Baker, 1998).

6. Westminster Shorter Catechism Q & A 26.

7. Jonathan Edwards, *Jonathan Edwards on Knowing Christ* (Carlisle, PA: Banner of Truth, 1990), 198-99.

Chapter 8

1. Evidence in support of this conclusion includes the fact that the prophet speaks of his 'stringed instruments' in Habakkuk 3:19 and that his prophecy displays psalm-like qualities, especially in chapters 1 and 3.

2. This is further evidence that Habakkuk may have been a Levite because he begins his prophecy much like a Psalm of Lament. Compare Habakkuk 1:2 with Psalms 6, 13, 79, 89, 90, and 94.

3. Willem VanGemeren, *Interpreting the Prophetic Word* (Grand Rapids, MI: Zondervan, 1990), 171.

4. From A.S. Peake, *The Heroes and Martyrs of the Faith*, as quoted in Donald A. Hagner, *Encoutering the Book of Hebrews* (Grand Rapids, MI: Baker Academic, 2002), 141.

5. Westminster Confession of Faith 14:2.

6. As you recall from the introduction to this book, the principle of escalation is when the 'antitype' (the New Testament fulfillment of the type) far exceeds the glory and import of the original type in the Old Testament. This principle reminds us that the New Testament realities far outshine their Old Testament shadows.

7. Robert Haldane, *Commentary on Romans* (Grand Rapids, MI: Kregel, 1988), 58.

8. As quoted in Bruce L. Shelley's *Church History in Plain Language* (Dallas, TX: Word, 1995), 239.

9. Edward Donnelly, 'By Faith Alone', *Banner of Truth*, Issue 479-80, August-September, 2003, page 46.

10. Actually, the Old Testament also reveals that the timing of the fulfillment of this prophecy is connected to the Messianic age. In the eleventh chapter of his prophecy, Isaiah employs language similar to that found in Habakkuk 2:14. Isaiah begins by referring directly to the coming of the Messiah: "A shoot will come up from the stump of Jesse; from his roots a Branch will bear fruit. The Spirit of the LORD will rest on him-- the Spirit of wisdom and of understanding, the Spirit of counsel and of power, the Spirit of knowledge and of the fear of the LORD," (Isaiah 11:1-2). After this introduction, Isaiah proceeds to explain that the Messiah's ministry will have global implications. He declares that when Jesus comes, '...the earth will be full of the knowledge of the LORD as the waters cover the sea' (Isaiah 11:9). Isaiah proclaims the worldwide spread of the knowledge of the Lord will coincide with the commencement of the kingdom of the Messiah.

11. John Murray, *Redemption Accomplished and Applied* (Grand Rapids, MI: Eerdmans, 1955), 110.

12. Westminster Confession of Faith 14:2.

13. As quoted in Edward Donnelly, 'By Faith Alone', *Banner of Truth*, Issue 479-80, August-September, 2003, page 45.

Chapter 9

1. In fact, some commentators speculate that Zephaniah's preaching may have sparked Josiah's reformation.

2. The Old Testament scholar Carl Friedrich Keil took this position noting that Zephaniah reproduced 'in a compendious form the fundamental thoughts of judgment and salvation which are common to all the prophets.' See C.F. Keil and F. Delitzsch, *Commentary on the Old Testament: Minor Prophets*, vol. 10 (Peabody, MA: Hendrickson, 1996), 437.

3. Commentator David W. Baker notes, 'The possible echo of Genesis 1…could indicate that the judgment portrayed here is to be seen as a reversal of creation. Man's sin leads to God's punishment, which in effect brings creation full-circle to where it was before God actively formed the universe. Light gives way to darkness, and the order of the well established creation reverts to disorder.' See David W. Baker, *Nahum, Habakkuk, Zephaniah: Tyndale Old Testament Commentaries*, vol. 23b, ed. D.J. Wiseman (Downers Grove, IL: IVP, 1988), 100-101.

4. Calling on the name of the Lord is an act of worship. See Genesis 4:26, 12:8, 13:4, 26:25 & Psalm 116:13 & 17.

5. Here we learn that redemption leads to holiness, not the other way around. O. Palmer Robertson commented as follows on this text: 'Now the prophet describes the consequences rather than the causes of the Lord's preserving a remnant…. The moral character of the remnant conforms to the nature of the Lord who has delivered them.' See O. Palmer Robertson, *Nahum, Habakkuk and Zephaniah: New International Commentary on the Old Testament*, ed. R.K. Harrison (Grand Rapids, MI: Eerdmans, 1990), 331.

6. It may be helpful at this point to explain that one of the rules for interpreting prophecy is the rule of 'progressive fulfillment'. Willem VanGemeren describes this principle as follows: 'The hermeneutics of progressive fulfillment looks at God's promises as a vine that grows, extends its branches in various directions, bears fruit, and keeps developing…. The promises of God cannot be reduced to predictions. A prediction limits the word to a particular fulfillment, whereas a promise unfolds progressively over time. A promise is like a rolling snowball in its momentum and significance.' Willem VanGemeren, *Interpreting the Prophetic Word* (Grand Rapids, MI: Zondervan, 1990), 83. This prin-

ciple corresponds to the "Way of Promise-Fulfillment" discussed in the introductory chapter.

7. See also Romans 2:16; Philippians 1:10; 2:16 and 2 Timothy 4:8.

8. Matthew Henry, *Matthew Henry's Commentary on the Whole Bible*, vol. 4 (Peabody, MA: Hendrickson, 1991), 1085.

9. While some commentators consider Zephaniah 3:9-10 to be solely referring to the return of dispersed Jews, this interpretation seems unlikely given the universal language contained in verses 9-10 and the fact that all nations are addressed in the verse immediately preceding this promise (v. 8). The context indicates that the substance of the promise is that God will draw his people from all nations.

10. Raymond B. Dillard and Tremper Longman's *An Introduction to the Old Testament* (Grand Rapids, MI: Zondervan, 1994), 420.

11. Most systematic theologians refer to this definitive break with sin as 'definitive sanctification'.

12. Compare this language to Revelation 21:3-5.

CHAPTER 10

1. The fact that Haggai's name is related to the word 'festival' is a good indication that he may have been born during one of Israel's festivals.

2. See Ezra 2:64-65 and Nehemiah 7:66-67.

3. See Ezra 4:4-5.

4. Willem VanGemeren, *Interpreting the Prophetic Word* (Grand Rapids, MI: Zondervan, 1990), 189.

5. There are some scholars who continue to claim that this is a direct reference to the Messiah. For example, see Walter C. Kaiser, Jr., *The Messiah in the Old Testament* (Grand Rapids, MI: Zondervan, 1995), 206-209. However, the Hebrew grammar indicates that while the noun "desired" is singular, the verb 'will come' is plural. This implies that the noun should be taken as a corporate noun.

6. It is interesting to note that Calvin believed Herod's improvements to the Temple was the work of Satan who was trying to deceive the Jews by making them look to the structure instead of the true spiritual temple present before them in Jesus Christ. See John Calvin, *Calvin's Commentaries*, vol. 15, trans. Thomas Myers (Grand Rapids, MI: Baker Books, 1989), 361-363.

7. John Calvin, *Calvin's Commentaries*, vol. 15, trans. Thomas Myers (Grand Rapids, MI: Baker Books, 1989), 364.

8. James Montgomery Boice, *The Minor Prophets*, vol. 2 (Grand Rapids, MI: Baker, 2003), 470.

9. Willem VanGemeren, *Interpreting the Prophetic Word* (Grand Rapids, MI: Zondervan, 1990), 189.

CHAPTER II

1. Source for quotation: Robert J. Morgan, *Nelson's Complete Book of Stories, Illustrations & Quotes* (Nashville, TN: Nelson, 2000), 435.

2. Raymond B. Dillard and Tremper Longman, III, *An Introduction to the Old Testament* (Grand Rapids, MI: Zondervan, 1994), 427.

3. Dillard and Longman, 427.

4. Dillard and Longman, 427.

5. Those narratives dealing with the suffering and death of Jesus Christ.

6. Dillard and Longman, 427.

7. Walter C. Kaiser, Jr., *The Messiah in the Old Testament* (Grand Rapids, MI: Zondervan, 1995), 211.

8. Willem VanGemeren, *Interpreting the Prophetic Word* (Grand Rapids, MI: Zondervan, 1990), 196.

9. For a helpful and accessible summary of the meaning of these visions, see Raymond B. Dillard and Tremper Longman, III, *An Introduction to the Old Testament* (Grand Rapids, MI: Zondervan, 1994), 433-435.

10. The Hebrew word for 'filthy' is related to the Hebrew word for human excrement.

11. See also Isaiah 49:1-7 and 52:13-53:12.

12. Zechariah also speaks of a 'cornerstone' coming from Judah in Zechariah 10:4. In addition, Stone imagery is also used to refer to the Messiah in the prophecy of Daniel (see Daniel 2:44-45).

13. Interestingly, Exodus 21:32 states that 30 pieces of silver was the price required to be paid to compensate a slave owner in the event that his slave was gored by another man's ox. Further evidence of the paltry nature of this payment is the phrase 'Throw it to the potter.' This phrase is equivalent to saying 'throw it away' because it is worthless.

14. C.F. Keil and F. Delitzsch, *Commentary on the Old Testament: Minor Prophets*, vol. 10 (Peabody, MA: Hendrickson, 1996), 615.

15. The prophet Isaiah expresses this same truth in his prophecy: 'Yet it was the LORD's will to crush him and cause him to suffer' (Isaiah 53:10).

16. It is important to remember that Jesus did not actually become sinful, but rather the sins of the elect were imputed to him; they were

charged to his account and he paid the penalty for them in his cruci-fixion.

17. D. Martyn Lloyd-Jones, *Spiritual Depression: Its Causes and Cure* (Grand Rapids, MI: Eerdmans, 1973), 90.

18. There is a debate regarding what, if anything, the donkey sym-bolizes in this text. I am persuaded that the donkey primarily symbol-izes the peace which accompanied the first advent of the Messiah. For a discussion of this issue see C.F. Keil and F. Delitzsch, *Commentary on the Old Testament: Minor Prophets*, vol. 10 (Peabody, MA: Hendrickson, 1996), 576-577. It is interesting to note that while the Messiah came on a donkey during his first advent, he will come on a war horse in his second advent (see Rev. 19:11).

19. VanGemeren, 201-202. All references in this quotation are to Zechariah's prophecy.

20. The power of this Messianic imagery of the Messiah riding on a donkey is further enhanced by the prophecy in Genesis 49:10-11 which gives the promise of a ruler coming from the tribe of Judah (David's tribe) who will 'tether his donkey to a vine, his colt to the choicest branch'.

21. Lloyd-Jones, 105.

CHAPTER 12

1. A similar construction occurs in Psalm 110: 'The LORD (*Yah-weh*) says to my Lord (*Adon*): "Sit at my right hand…"' (Psalm 110:1). Again, the point is to demonstrate the relationship between God the Father and God the Son. Jesus used this text in the Gospels as evidence of his divinity and Messianic role (see Matthew 22:41-46). The apostle Peter also uses it for a similar purpose (see Acts 2:32-36). While the word *Adon* may be used to refer to an earthly master, the Hebrew gram-matical construction found in Malachi 3:1 indicates a reference to the divine lord. See Walter C. Kaiser, Jr., *The Messiah in the Old Testament* (Grand Rapids, MI: Zondervan, 1995), 228.

2. See Hebrews 8:6; 9:15; 12:24.

3. Kaiser, 228.

4. While Malachi 3:3 seems to imply that this purification is only for the Levites, most commentators agree that this work of the Messiah extends to all of his people. After all, the New Testament reminds us that each member of the New Covenant community is part of a 'royal priesthood' and a 'holy nation' (1 Peter 2:9).

Jonathan Edwards: The Holy Spirit In Revival

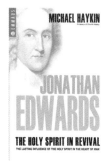

ISBN: 0 85234 599 2

Jonathan Edwards could arguably be called America's greatest theologian. His ministry in eighteenth-century New England was one of the chief means that the Spirit of God used to spark revivals in Northampton and the surrounding area – and eventually what is known as the Great Awakening. These sweeping revivals brought many souls to Christ and Edwards' ongoing ministry and extensive writings continued to have an impact on many others, both in America and throughout Europe.

Michael Haykin's study of Jonathan Edwards is interwoven with an acute understanding of both the primary texts – such as Edwards' landmark study of Christian spirituality, The Religious Affections – and the historical context. Drawing on both of these, he presents a detailed analysis of the shape and content of Edwards' theology, including an examination of his wife's experience of revival and his daughter's reflections on it. Jonathan Edwards had a heart devoted to the pursuit of the glory of God and this volume reflects something of that passion.

Dr Michael A. G. Haykin is Principal of Toronto Baptist Seminary, Toronto, Ontario, Canada, and a Senior Fellow of The Jonathan Edwards Centre for Reformed Spirituality, Toronto. He also serves as Adjunct Professor of Church History at The Southern Baptist Theological Seminary, Louisville, Kentucky, USA. Michael is a popular conference speaker in North America and the UK and has written and edited numerous books including Defence of the truth *and* One heart and one soul. *Michael is married to Alison and they have two children.*

The Gospel Ministry

ISBN: 0 85234 595 X

Practical insights and application

Editor: Philip H. Eveson

Evangelist, pastor, teacher – today's gospel minister juggles several different roles. As Andrew A. Davies says in his paper, 'Pastoring the flock of God in today's world is a challenging business. This is partly because the pastoral office itself is under attack, partly because professionals have taken over pastoral functions, and partly because pastors have to deal with an often-bewildering variety of pastoral difficulties.' From the biblical foundations of gospel preaching through a historical review of pastoral ministry to a look at ministry in the context of contemporary society, the contributors to this book evaluate the work of gospel ministry, explore in detail the roles of pastor, teacher and evangelist, and conclude with an examination of ministerial training.

Philip Eveson is a Welshman who has studied the biblical languages and theology at the University of Wales, Cambridge and London. He has been the minister of Kensit Evangelical Church for twenty-five years and is now the Principal of the London Theological Seminary, where he has lectured since its inception. Philip Eveson is also the author of The Book of Origins – Genesis simply explained, part of the ever-popular Welwyn Commentary Series.

Rapture Fiction and the Evangelical Crisis

ISBN: 0 85234 610 7

"Jesus Christ will soon return to the earth. This book, like the rapture fiction novels it discusses, finds its hope in that statement's truth. Nothing that this book argues should therefore be understood as in any way underplaying the significance of our Lord's second coming, or its central importance in consistent Christian living. The New Testament documents shine with the anticipation of glory, and this book must not dull that hope.

Rapture Fiction and the Evangelical Crisis seeks to retain rapture novels' enthusiasm for the return of Jesus Christ at the same time as it examines their presentation of the gospel. Its most basic argument is that rapture novels have emerged from an evangelicalism that shows signs of serious theological decay. In their descriptions of conversion and Christian living, rapture fiction novels demonstrate a sometimes inadequate understanding of the gospel, the church and the Christian life. These novels are some of the best-selling 'evangelical' titles in the world, but the faith they represent cannot be identified with the historic orthodoxy of evangelical Protestantism, the 'faith which was once delivered unto the saints' (Jude 3). The novels' combination of theological inadequacy and massive popularity is evidence that evangelicalism is now in serious crisis."

Crawford Gribben is the lecturer in Renaissance literature and culture at the University of Manchester, a member of the Evangelical Presbyterian Church, and the author of The Irish Puritans: James Ussher and the Reformation of the Church *(Evangelical Press).*

Living in the Hope of Future Glory

ISBN: 0 85234 608 2

The Glorification of the Christian

A decade ago Tom Barnes began to collect information and take notes of statements in the Bible which would relate to the doctrine of glorification. He decided that someday he would study glorification thoroughly for the purpose of his own growth and for that of teaching his own congregation.

The results of what he found had such a profound impact on him that he decided to share them with a wider audience. This book is the result. The purpose of this book is that as you read this work your faith in our great Lord and his work in your life will be strengthened, that you will come to see with greater clarity the hope of your calling, that you will be moved to worship our Saviour, and finally that your life will become a billboard for the glory of our sovereign God!

God created mankind with glory, full and rich weightiness, a significance that consisted of being made in his image. Man reflects God in a way that none of the rest of creation can; his very purpose is to glorify God, to live in him forever. But when man fell into sin, part of that image was twisted and man fell from glory.

Tom Barnes, a Theology instructor at the Dayspring Center For Christian Studies and senior pastor of Living Hope Evangelical Free Church, is a graduate of Liberty University in Lynchburg, Virginia (B.S.), Trinity Evangelical Divinity School in Deerfield, Illinois (M.Div), and Bethel Theological Seminary in St. Paul, Minnesota (D.Min.). Tom lives in Ft. Collins, Colorado, USA with his wife, Karen, and their three children.

A wide range of excellent books on spiritual subjects is available from Evangelical Press. Please write to us for your free catalogue or contact us by e-mail.

Evangelical Press
Faverdale North, Darlington, Co. Durham, DL3 OPH, England
email: sales@evangelicalpress.org

Evangelical Press USA
P. O. Box 825, Webster, NY 14580, USA
email: usa.sales@evangelicalpress.org

web: http://www.evangelicalpress.org